ENJOYING TRADITIONAL JAZZ

By

Pops Coffee

Copyright © 2016

Table of Contents

2

Introduction

This book is for anyone who enjoys the foot-tapping pleasure of listening to traditional jazz, whether you are a musician or not. It is neither a history nor an encyclopedia of the music. You can find such things elsewhere.

What I am offering you is a collection of articles in which I try to share my enthusiasm for the music and pass on what I have discovered about it. I hope you will find something of interest wherever you choose to dip into it.

I became seriously interested in traditional jazz when I was about fifty years old. From that age, I worked quite hard at learning to play it on the trumpet. I wish I had done this when I was younger. However, I reached a fair standard and ended up as a member of a couple of bands. This book is based largely on what I have discovered, mainly as a result of listening to bands (mostly on internet videos) and visiting New Orleans, which has become the best place in the world to hear the music.

To illustrate the points I am making, I include links to videos on the internet.

It happens on rare occasions that someone puts up a video and at a later date chooses to remove it. Obviously I have no control over this. I'm sorry if it happens to any of the videos I have recommended. They are all available at the time of writing.

SECTION 1: ENJOY!

Right away, before we start talking too seriously about the music, I want to invite you to enjoy some of the music that has brought me so much pleasure in my old age.

A GREAT VIDEO

Please watch this great YouTube video - one of the the best and most exciting, sizzling, energetic performances of New Orleans traditional jazz to appear in the last few years. It runs for half an hour, with high-definition pictures and top-quality sound. So just settle to this marvellous little concert that will bring tears of joy to the eyes of any traditional jazz lover.

It's *The Shotgun Jazz Band* playing *Climax Rag*, *Love Songs of the Nile*, *Oriental Man*, *I Can't Escape*, *Yearning* and *Mobile Stomp.*

This is raw New Orleans jazz at its best. Leader Marla Dixon stamps her dynamic personality on everything. She is flanked by great players - James Evans (from Beaumaris, Wales) on reeds and Barnabus Jones on trombone. All three of them are on terrific form and their ensemble work is an example to us all. But this band also has the perfect rhythm section - Tyler Thompson on bass, John Dixon on banjo, and Justin Peake on drums. John Dixon kindly let me know that Tyler's favourite string bass player is Slow Drag Pavageau and that John's own banjo hero was George Guesnon. John added that they were both 'solid 4/4 players'. He told me the 'genesis of *The Shotgun* was via the *Happy Pals* in Toronto which has become the incubator for some great musicians. Marla and Tyler both got the start there. *The Happy Pals* were directly influenced by the Kid Thomas band, so that 4/4 revival beat of Sammy Penn is also a large influence.'

That explains a lot. The Shotgun Band gives an extraordinary demonstration of just how New Orleans-style rhythm backing should be. Justin Peake is a drummer about whom I know virtually nothing. But it seems he was led to this style of music by the Dixons themselves. On the evidence of this Abita Springs performance I would rate him right up there with the best.

Enough of this. Get on to the video here:

https://www.youtube.com/watch?v=RicINWvmAcg#t=232

And now I must tell you I woke up to an amazing treat on the morning of 17 June 2016.

There was a brand-new video on YouTube, filmed three days earlier by James Sterling, of The Shotgun Jazz Band playing *Canal Street Blues*.

But what brought a huge smile to my face was that it starts with a dedication to ME! Marla introduces it by saying it is for their 'friend in the U.K. - Ivan'!

Not only that; Marla then goes on to lead the band in a terrific performance of this King Oliver classic. She drives everyone through more than a dozen varied and exciting ensemble choruses. She uses her mute and flattened thirds in the most thrilling fashion. Tom Fischer on clarinet makes a great job of the famous Johnny Dodds' solo choruses. And they even end with that super-neat little Oliver coda.

But I hope you will watch it for yourself. Do so by going here:

https://www.youtube.com/watch?v=bR5hNy1i8mo

This will become one of my all-time favourite videos!

JAMES EVANS, CHLOE FEORANZO - AND A MAGICAL MOMENT

During my April 2016 visit to New Orleans, one moment stood out as the most wonderful and magical. There were four choruses of amazing improvisation at the end of a performance of *Bye Bye Blues* in which two really great musicians produced the most exciting two minutes of music I have ever heard.

I was in the audience at The Spotted Cat on Saturday 9 April. Chloe Feoranzo, the great young clarinet and saxophone player (and singer) had moved to New Orleans only a few days earlier and had not yet even finished unpacking her belongings. But she was already sitting in with some bands and booked to play in others.

With so many musicians engaged elsewhere in French Quarter Festival duties, The Shotgun Jazz Band was short of its regular staff: they had no trombone player. So the brilliant James Evans (like Chloe, one of the world's greatest traditional jazz reed players and also a very good singer) switched to trombone for some numbers (yes, he can play that instrument very well too!). And Chloe played the full gig on reeds.

When we reached the final number of the second set, Marla Dixon left the stand to go among the audience with the 'tips bucket' as she always does. This left James and Chloe in charge of the music. So they chose *Bye Bye Blues*, <u>both using their C Melody Saxes</u>.

Thank goodness video-maker James Sterling was there! He had driven over from Florida and was filming it on his mobile phone. Thanks to James, you too can now witness (on YouTube) this very special performance.

It is astonishing to think that only four musicians were involved (two of them on saxes) and that such pulsating music resulted. We have John Dixon on banjo and Tyler Thomson on string bass (in my opinion the best combination in the world, when it comes to driving music along in a rock-steady 4/4). The piece starts off normally enough with James Evans introducing the melody. The excitement gradually builds up. Note what happens at 2 minutes 55 seconds, after John Dixon's chorus. James and Chloe play one chorus 'trading eights' and then one 'trading fours' and then another 'trading twos'. Absolutely thrilling. It is amazing what is produced by James Evans and this young lady half his age. Just look at the faces of James Evans and Tyler Thompson. They knew something very special was going on. Finally, there is a throbbing 'all-in' chorus in which the two sax players are positively bouncing in their seats. I can tell you the audience loved it and there were tears of joy in the eyes of seasoned veterans.

Now turn up the volume and judge for yourself:
https://www.youtube.com/watch?v=rTFXYDyBRr4

I spent quite a bit of time with the video-maker James Sterling and his wife Markay during my visit and I can tell you he is a wonderful and generous gentleman.

MARLA DIXON AND 'OVER IN THE GLORYLAND'

While I am on the subject of *The Shotgun Jazz Band*, let me tell you it is one of the most exciting bands playing traditional jazz anywhere in the world at the moment. The band is led in New Orleans by Marla Dixon, who moved there from Toronto in Canada. Examples of their work on YouTube have been thrilling. The band has been in existence and evolving since about 2009 but I think with the house style and personnel it arrived at by 2015, it achieved new heights. As their own website says:

With an emphasis on ensemble playing, a stomping rhythm section, and a genuine love of the hot, bluesy, no-frills melodies that once poured forth from New Orleans' dance halls, Shotgun Jazz Band makes music that is both immediate in its influences and timeless in its appeal.

One of the videos on YouTube shows them playing *Over In The Gloryland*, the 1920 song by Acuff and Dean. You can watch it here:

https://www.youtube.com/watch?v=NMNOfxQ7qG8

Some musicians are not keen on this tune because they say it has a dreary chord structure, with an over-dependence on the home chord of Ab. But Marla and her team show how thrilling it can be. In Marla's playing we experience raw New Orleans jazz at its best.

One of the devices that helps create this rawness is the use of flattened thirds above the chords. (By the way, a banjo-playing friend tells me it might be better to think of these flattened thirds as 'flattened 10ths', as this conveys the fact that they are played *above* the chord.)

Notice the wonderful effect these notes have at precisely 4 mins 49 seconds and at 6 minutes 56 seconds. In both cases, during an Eb7 chord, Marla plays (and bends) a high Gb. I guess she does this instinctively and does not have think 'I'll put in a flattened third here and see how it sounds.'

'PERCOLATIN' BLUES'

Percolatin' Blues was written in about 1925 by Lemuel Fowler.

He was a composer of 57 tunes and an important pianist. He featured in many early jazz recordings. *Percolatin' Blues* was recorded by the great blues singer Clara Smith in 1926, with Fowler himself at the piano.

It was a fine modern video on YouTube that brought me to this song. I chanced upon *The Smoking Time Jazz Club* with their radiant singer Sarah Peterson giving a performance of *Percolatin' Blues* in a New Orleans street. Compared with the original, they simplify the Verse down to one set of 16 bars only.

The film (in HD) was made by Beau Patrick Coulon and his team. The video is of the highest professional quality: a splendid range of shots takes us all round the band and the street dancers with great attention to detail. You watch this video and immediately want to get on the next plane to New Orleans. The joyful atmosphere is so infectious. These are people who know how to have a good time. Here's where to watch it:

https://www.youtube.com/watch?v=dfuHwPtVQOc

VIDEOS SHORT AND SWEET

Which would be your three *most joyful* short YouTube videos. Here are mine.

NUMBER ONE
The best traditional jazz band in the world (from New Orleans but performing in Switzerland) plays a particularly thrilling tune. The excitement builds and builds!
https://www.youtube.com/watch?v=J_jB_WbPg9I

NUMBER TWO
Star buskers are in Asheville, North Carolina. The composer himself sings the song and plays the fiddle. And the three charming ladies among the five musicians exude happiness.
https://www.youtube.com/watch?v=nEmU3E8rras

NUMBER THREE
Pure enjoyment! About fifteen New Orleans street musicians get together in a bar one evening to play and sing *Round and Round*, a fun song created by Charlie Nickerson and the Memphis Jug Band in 1930. I can't resist singing along:
https://www.youtube.com/watch?v=_3NSAlr0On4

CHLOE, ALBANIE, HARRY WOODS - 'WHAT A LITTLE MOONLIGHT CAN DO'

May I recommend a lovely video to you? It was filmed by James Sterling of Florida when he spent a weekend in New Orleans during June 2016.

Like me, James is a fan of Chloe Feoranzo and Albanie Falletta, so, when he heard that they had recently got together and would be playing with Kaladeva Chandra and John Joyce in a quartet at the dba music club in Frenchmen Street, he eagerly went to see them.

James requested one of his favourites - *What a Little Moonlight Can Do*. They told him they had never played it together before. However, after a little chat among themselves about how to tackle it and in which key, off they went.

The result is so good. All four musicians are brilliant and Albanie's singing is utterly charming. Watch the performance here:

https://www.youtube.com/watch?v=qyooxaRZBmI

By the way, *What a Little Moonlight Can Do* was composed (both words and music) in 1934 by Harry Woods. He wrote it for the movie *Road House*, which was filmed in England while Harry was working for a brief spell in London. It was sung in the movie by Violet Lorraine.

What a phenomenal contribution Harry made to our music: *The Clouds Will Soon Roll By, I Wish't I Was in Peoria, I'm Looking Over a Four-Leaf Clover, Paddlin' Madeline Home, River - Stay Away From My Door, Side By Side, That's All There Is - There Ain't No More; Try a Little Tenderness, We Just Couldn't Say Goodbye, When Somebody Thinks You're Wonderful, When the*

18

Moon Comes Over the Mountain, When the Red Red Robin Comes Bob Bob Bobbin' Along, - all of these are examples of the songs he composed.

Harry Woods lived from 1896 until 1970. Two sad points about him are these: he was born without fingers on his left hand; and he died when knocked down by a car right outside his house in Glendale, Arizona.

What a Little Moonlight Can Do is a little unusual. Most popular songs of this kind were at the time constructed in 32 bars, usually consisting of four sets of 8 bars. Harry Woods has 'doubled up' in the structure of this song. There are four sets of 16 bars, making 64 bars in total. The first 32 bars have much in common with the second 32. In fact, Bars 1 - 11 are Bars 33 - 43 are identical in melody and chord structure.

'I CHARLESTON' VIDEOS

Just in case you are one of those people who have not come across the life-affirming, heart-warming 'I Charleston' videos, I must tell you that you have missed a treat. Do something about it and take a look at them. What happens is that a group of enthusiasts (mostly young) make a video in which they energetically dance in settings that highlight the sights and architecture and tourist attractions of their city.

It is great fun and mildly competitive. You can decide for yourself which city has made the best video. For traditional jazz fans, there's the added attraction that many of the videos use good recordings of our bands as the accompaniment to the dancers.

There are plenty of these videos on YouTube. You might care to start with New York City by going to this one:

https://www.youtube.com/watch?v=bB40NcumOOs

Warsaw has even used music by our beloved Tuba Skinny to provide the accompaniment:

https://www.youtube.com/watch?v=wjI7_xEFcPA

ICE MAN

One of the 2013 videos of Tuba Skinny, brought to us by the generous *digitalalexa*, is a performance of *Ice Man*. The band is playing for fun, outdoors, late on a warm summer evening. It is almost completely dark.

You can watch the performance here:

https://www.youtube.com/watch?v=pCfdF6g2vG0

I had never heard of *Ice Man* (but have discovered there were several tunes of this title: one was written and recorded by Memphis Minnie in 1936). The one played by Tuba Skinny, however, is believed to be an old Cajun music theme, composer unknown. It is one of the most delightful and infectious music performances you will come across. Six members of the band are present and they are totally relaxed, making music just to please themselves and for the sheer joy of it.

Ice Man is essentially a simple eight-bar theme, using just the tonic and dominant chords. It's the kind of tune that could have been composed on the back of an envelope in about 15 minutes. Maybe it was!

My guess is that this was Tuba Skinny's first-ever performance of it. The context and treatment suggest that it was played at the request of (and led by) the guitarist, who was the only one who knew the words of the spoken 'verses'. The fact that they play it in the key of G (usually considered awkward for Bb brass instruments) supports the theory that the key was chosen to please the guitarist.

Tuba Skinny show us what can be achieved even with such simple material. Notice the perfect line laid down by Todd Burdick's tuba. Enjoy Robin's use of the full range of his percussion, including the makeshift cymbal. And note how the two of them work smartly together at each 'cut-off' point. Enjoy the close-harmony singing of the two ladies (Shaye and Erika). Admire Barnabus's usual creative work on the trombone. And note as always Shaye's magical work on the cornet - a perfect bluesy 8 bars at 2 mins 50 secs, and her astonishing colouring behind the brief trombone solo at 1 min 49 secs.

SHAYE'S ALL-LADIES BAND

In the summer of 2016, Shaye Cohn put together in New Orleans a six-piece traditional jazz band comprising only ladies. We are lucky to live at a time when so many of the greatest traditional jazz musicians are ladies and when so many of them happen to have settled in that city.

Shaye's original purpose, I believe, was simply to give a demonstration of traditional jazz at the Girls' Summer Band Camp in New Orleans. But the all-ladies band - once formed - was too good to waste and fans pleaded for them to play elsewhere.

At first, the band had no name but somebody (John Dixon, I believe) had the idea of calling it *The EQP Jazz Band* (EQual Pay). However, by November, Shaye seems to have decided to call it *The Shake 'Em Up Jazz Band*.

Whatever the band's name, the Good News is that they were invited to play at the famous Abita Springs Opry on 19 November 2016.

The concert they gave was traditional jazz of the finest kind - tasteful and yet always exciting and full of intelligent ideas. They opened with *Some Day Sweetheart* and then continued with *Root, Hog; or Die!*, *Sugar Blues*, *When You Wore A Tulip*, *Make Me A Pallet on the Floor*, and - to finish - *Hindustan*.

Having done the good work behind the scenes, Shaye gave herself a secondary role in performance, leaving Marla to play the trumpet, lead the band and do the announcing.

Everyone was interested to see how Shaye would fare playing her newest instrument, the trombone. Already known as a great multi-instrumentalist and one of the best jazz musicians in the world, Shaye had only recently taken up this instrument.

What she did was what we might expect of her: she played a perfect and accurate though simple and basic line. On *Sugar Blues* (played in the rarely-used key of G) she took a complete solo chorus and the audience loved it.

Root, Hog; Or Die! - played in C minor - romped along, with plenty of mini-solos and Marla providing the vocal.

Among the highlights of the concert were a beautiful two-chorus solo by Chloe on *Make Me a Pallet* (which they played in F) and an exquisite vocal duet at the end of *When You Wore A Tulip* (played in Ab) with Chloe singing the melody and Marla perfectly harmonising on lower notes. Chloe was also the vocalist on *Sugar Blues*, which she sang with great passion.

(I am mentioning some of the keys because they differ from those often used for the tunes in question.)

Pumping the band along, Molly on guitar and Julie on string bass provided the chords very solidly, four to the bar; and Dizzy as ever maintained metronomic gentle percussion on the washboard, and took very neat solos, including a full chorus on *When You Wore a Tulip*.

Molly is, of course, also a fine singer and gave a lovely rendition of *Make Me a Pallet*.

Chloe's clarinet was stunningly eloquent throughout and Marla was her usual exuberant self – passionately singing and also playing some wonderful stuff on the trumpet. On this occasion she did not use her famous Derby mute but her playing with the plunger mute on *Sugar Blues* and *Pallet on the Floor* was outstanding.

What a treat for us all! Let's hope this band will continue to get together from time to time and that there will be many more videos for us to enjoy all over the world.

You should be able to watch the Abita Springs video of the performance by going to Abita Spring's own site:

http://www.abitaopry.org/html/AO2016-11.html

and then clicking on the name of the band.

It is also to be seen here:

https://vimeo.com/201161078

THE NEPTUNE BAND - A DELIGHT

In late 2016, I first came across videos of *The Neptune Band* of Zimbabwe. This band no longer exists but it flourished over 30 years ago. It was exceptional in being an authentic-sounding 'early New Orleans' style band based not in New Orleans but in the heart of Africa. It was also exceptional in that it was made up of four children from one family, their teacher and his teenage son.

Although this band was a new discovery for me, my friend John Whitehorn told me he heard the band in the 1980s and he kindly supplied me with some information about them.

So here's the story.

The Band was created by a gentleman called Cesar Jose Fratantoni. A dentist by profession, he was of Italian descent but grew up in Argentina. He mastered the clarinet and piano and was devoted to New Orleans jazz, particularly collecting and learning from the recordings of King Oliver and Jelly Roll Morton. He moved to Africa in 1971 and took a great interest in African music. Later he adopted into his household five children - Sabina Siankope (who became the band's banjo player) and her four brothers. They helped in the household and he helped them with their education and trained them as *The Neptune Band*, with his own son - Stephen Cesar Fratantoni - on cornet.

They practised together for two hours every day, with only Mr. Fratantoni and his piano to guide them. (My guess is that Mr. Fratantoni himself had purchased all the instruments.) In 1981, following four such years of hard work, Mr. Fratantoni was determined to take his 'family band' to New Orleans, so that they could be heard there and also learn from the other musicians in the

City. He had to obtain a huge overdraft from his bank to fund the trip.

So (with its drummer aged only 11 and its cornet player 15!) the Band went to New Orleans, where it gave some concerts, even including one in Preservation Hall. It was extremely well received. The great Allan Jaffe, who owned and developed Preservation Hall, was impressed.

And the Mayor of New Orleans formally conferred on The Neptune Band the status of Honorary Citizen.

The Band went on to play at the Breda Festival in the Netherlands in 1981 and also performed in Hanover, Germany, in 1984.

It is Mr. Fratantoni himself who in recent years has put several of the band's recordings on YouTube. Try *Chattanooga Stomp*, recorded when the band was in New Orleans in 1981:

https://www.youtube.com/watch?v=qYO3jfSQ9O0

Have you ever heard such a delightful, gentle performance?

The members of the band, in addition to Mr. Fratantoni himself on clarinet, were Triwell Sianjkope (17, bass), Sabina Violet Siankope (25, banjo and vocals), Daniel Ndoga Siankope (19, trombone), Stephen Cesar Fratantoni (15, cornet) and Japhet Sikeba Siankope (only 11, brilliant, especially for one so young at the time - percussion).

Mr. Fratantoni obviously set out with a clear policy to play authentic early New Orleans jazz, with plenty of melody, no exhibitionism, strong team-work and ensuring that all instruments could be clearly heard. The effect is that the playing sounds very simple, though of course this simplicity is deceptive. The emphasis is on ensemble playing rather than prima donna solos. Fratantoni himself said in an interview: 'For me this music is like the baroque

Italian music. It is classical. You know classical music is often very simple and it is often difficult to play because it is so simple.' We know exactly what he meant. They played the music with restraint and respectfully – respectful of the music itself and also of each other: that is what - for me at least - makes the sound of this band delightful and distinctive.

The banjo and bass players are very solid; and the 11-year-old on the drums could serve as a model for anyone wishing to become a percussionist in a traditional jazz band.

For a historic recording where we see them (in Preservation Hall!) playing *Tiger Rag* in a gentle manner, the like of which you may never have come across before:

https://www.youtube.com/watch?v=UjfmVOK8DdY

It is amazing to think how young they were. How well Mr. Fratantoni had trained them!

You can hear them playing *Careless Love Blues* in Lyon, France, in 1986:

https://www.youtube.com/watch?v=dxjUpZyjC8k

This performance is again remarkable for the apparent simplicity of the music and also for including the 12-bar Verse which many bands omit.

You can find several other videos of the band on YouTube.

This is traditional jazz the way I like it. Discovering this band with its wonderful young musicians has brought me pleasure; and I hope it is a pleasure you will also share.

TUBA SKINNY'S CD 'OWL CALL BLUES'

Tuba Skinny's friend (and frequent guitarist) Max Bien-Kahn recorded the music for the CD 'Owl Call Blues' over several days in one of the New Orleans houses in which Tuba Skinny musicians live. The resulting acoustic is of a very high quality.

Here's what the CD contains:

1. Crazy 'Bout You: a standard Tuba Skinny performance of the pleasant, simple 16-bar tune, with singing by Erika and good ensemble work. I enjoyed Shaye's cheeky Ab on the very last note played - turning the final chord into Bb7th!

2. Rosa Lee Blues: vocal by Greg (abetted by Erika) in this 12-bar blues, which is slightly unusual in having an eight-to-the-bar rhythm and being played in the key of G.

3. Cannonball Blues: An amazing key-changing 12-bar blues with a terrific arrangement. I love the moment when Shaye shakes her cornet though about 12 notes in half a second while changing the key from Eb to Ab! And it's clever how they slide down to the Key of C for Todd's tuba chorus before sliding up again to Ab.

4. Got a Mind To Ramble: One of those Erika vocals that we all love. Essentially a simple 8-bar theme in Bb - just the sort of material out of which nobody can make more than Erika and Tuba Skinny do.

5. Short-Dress Gal: Many of us know and love the 1927 original by the Sam Morgan Band. Tuba Skinny recreate it with their usual skill and Barnabus does a great job on the trombone, in the style of Big Jim Robinson on the Sam Morgan recording.

6. Owl Call Blues: I think for many of us this haunting song alone is worth the price of the CD. Shaye and Erika composed it; and here the band performs it lyrically for us.

7. Too Tight: The bouncy 16-bar blues highlights the strings and also Todd on the tuba.

8. Oriental Strut: Johnny St. Cyr's complex multi-part 1926 composition is very well executed, with a typical Tuba Skinny arrangement including some tricky breaks and rhythmic effects.

9. Ambulance Man: This 1930 Hattie Hart song is a duet with a story to tell. There is very good ensemble support. Basically a 12-bar Chorus in Bb but with a preceding Verse.

10. How Do They Do It That Way?: This Victoria Spivey song from 1929 is a favourite with the band and their followers. There are plenty of videos of them performing it. And I believe it's the only number they have recorded twice for CDs: it was also on their *Garbage Man* CD. So we are in familiar territory, though with a new arrangement. On this occasion they have chosen to play one Chorus in Eb and then one in Bb (Erika's preferred key) before Erika's vocal solo. But they return to Eb for a remarkable final Chorus, displaying Shaye's talents as she plays almost the entire Chorus against stop chords.

11. Dallas Rag: This tune (devised and recorded by The Dallas String Band in 1927) has settled into Tuba Skinny's repertoire. Although it's based on a simple chord sequence, given its liveliness and the use of breaks, it is a great fun number. Good work all round. Fans of Robin will enjoy hearing him strut his stuff.

12. Untrue Blues: Another 8-bar theme bouncily played and well sung by Erika. You'll enjoy hearing Shaye playing the fiddle here. Like Rosa Lee Blues (above) it's played in G.

13. Somebody's Been Lovin' My Baby: One of those sad tales that suits Erika's voice very well. A 32-bar song. Sounds like another example of a key that is hardly ever ventured into by other traditional jazz bands - A minor.

14. Willie the Weeper: Jazz bands have been playing this one since 1920. Tuba Skinny give a lusty creative performance, almost entirely with full ensemble and preferring the keys of G minor and Bb to those used by many bands - D minor and F. (Percussionist Robin told me this is his favourite track on the CD).

15. Travellin' Blues: A standard 12-bar, with Shaye on fiddle and Greg providing the vocal - again abetted by Erika.

TUBA SKINNY'S CD 'BLUE CHIME STOMP'

This CD was recorded at The Tigermen Den in Royal Street, New Orleans. Mr. Google shows me the building is situated in a peaceful spot about three-quarters of a mile east of the French Quarter. It is a restored 1830s corner store. It seems there is plenty of music and dancing there these days, and that great food is served.

Maybe the aim was to get an appropriate 'old-time dance hall' type of acoustic. (You may remember The Shotgun Jazz Band did just that with the CD they recorded in the former Luthjens Dance Hall.)

There is certainly a good sound quality to this CD. As soon as it begins, with a lusty performance of *Maple Leaf Rag*, you realise you can hear the tones of all the individual instruments very clearly. Turn up the volume and it's like having them in the room with you.

You later find that, in the recording process, Erika's voice has fared just a little less well in a couple of numbers than the instruments. She is a wonderful singer in great form and beloved by us all but listen to her performance of her own composition *Broken-Hearted Blues* on the band's 2009 CD and then listen to her performance of the same song on this 2016 CD. A big difference, isn't there? In the 2009 version, the voice is completely clear and you can make out all the words easily; but you can't *quite* say the same about this 2016 version.

The band has evolved, of course. In 2009, they had just five musicians, plus Erika singing. But in the 2016 CD, they sometimes use nine musicians (three of them reed men) in addition to Erika.

32

This has made Tuba Skinny sound more like a 'big band' on a few numbers. Especially when they use a driving saxophone and 'walking' riffs (as in *Running Down My Man* and *Broken-Hearted Blues*) we are in the realms of R&B music. Indeed the Tuba Skinny website - introducing this CD - stated '...*this album features us in a couple different line-ups - our traditional one, as well as one with multiple reed players, and also our R&B line-up including piano, upright bass and drum set*'.

There is also a greater sense of choreography these days. In the more complicated multi-theme tunes, such as *Soudan*, *Oh Papa*, Shaye's composition *Blue Chime Stomp*, the vigorous *Variety Stomp* and - to a lesser extent - *Dear Almanzoer*, all the musicians had to master their parts meticulously in order to participate in the strict, tight arrangements. Of course there is still room for free expression and improvising, but the backbone of each of these pieces is rigid.

Robin Rapuzzi (who - before playing washboard regularly with Tuba Skinny - was originally a complete percussionist) plays the full drum-kit on some of these numbers. Todd Burdick apparently plays the string bass rather than the tuba on some - but I have yet to work out which, though I think they include *Running Down My Man*. He told me last April that he had been 'learning to play a string bass' but he did not mention that he had already recorded with it!

The barrel-house piano, presumably the one belonging to The Tigermen Den, is played by Shaye on some of the pieces. One of these - *I'm Blue and Lonesome* - is heard in the key of Gb. Amazing. When did you last hear a tune performed by a jazz band in Gb? I can't recall when. All other bands would simply have opted for a key of G or F to keep the playing simpler.

And on the same subject, Erika sings *Running Down My Man* (the Merline Johnson 12-bar from 1936) in E - a key most traditional jazz musicians steer clear of.

These two tunes make me suspect the house piano was half a tone flat. After all, in YouTube videos (with Shaye on cornet rather than piano) they have always played *Running Down My Man* in F and *I'm Blue and Lonesome* in G. But for the CD Shaye switched to the piano. If, as I believe, it was half a tone flat, then its F actually produced an E and its G sounded like Gb. Perhaps that's the complete explanation. The band did very well to adapt to such awkward keys.

With very neat banjo support, Erika sings *Me and My Chauffeur* (the song written by E. Lawler and recorded in 1941 by Memphis Minnie). This is trickier to sing than it may sound: note the long pause that has to be left in the ninth and tenth bars. There are some gems from Erika - not only those I have mentioned but also the 12-bar blues (composed in the 1930s by Ann Turner for Georgia White) *Almost Afraid To Love*, and *Oh Papa* (the Ma Rainey number from 1927) and *Midnight Blues*, both with substantial vocals.

Anyone who has watched the YouTube videos of Tuba Skinny to emerge since March 2015 will have heard all of the tunes on this CD, so they may already be familiar to you.

But here are a few more thoughts about some of the pieces.

Soudan started out in about 1906 a a sort of tone poem for piano by the Czech composer Gabriel Sebek. He called it *Oriental Scene for Piano, Opus 45*. The sub-title was *In The Soudan: A Dervish Chorus*. The ODJB recorded an adaptation of it in 1917 as *Oriental Jazz* (or *Jass*) and recorded it again in 1920 - this time as *Soudan*. As I have indicated, Tuba Skinny play a neat, strict arrangement. Their version intersperses the 'oriental' theme in F minor with the more bouncy traditional theme in the related key of Ab, and there is a trombone-led F minor coda from Barnabus to round it off. It's a very unusual number!

Corrine (sung by Erika) is *not* the same as the famous *Corrine Corrina. Corrine,* recorded in 1937 by Blind Boy Fuller, is a 16-bar blues, not a 12-bar. Erika gives a fine performance in the key of A, appropriately supported by the resonator guitar.

Memphis Shake (long-since established in Tuba Skinny's repertoire) is a straightforward number of two short themes and distinctive diminished chords. The 'big band' line-up gives it a delightfully free treatment, with much ensemble work.

Similar is *Shake It And Break It* (which has two short themes - in minor and major keys). The performance is very enjoyable and the final minutes are taken up with some pretty soloing and ensemble on the major-key theme.

Blue Chime Stomp is of course yet another fine composition by Shaye.

The CD ends with a very pleasant and straightforward version of *Chloe* - bringing things full circle in a sense, as this number also featured sweetly on their very first CD of seven years earlier, when they had only five musicians: a cornet, violin and trombone were supported merely by a tuba and guitar. This latest CD version of *Chloe* (using at least eight musicians) is taken a shade more slowly.

I must also mention the order in which the tunes have been thoughtfully arranged on the CD: fast and slow numbers alternate, as do instrumentals and vocals. So, played straight through, it makes a good concert.

'TAKE ME OUT TO THE BALL GAME'

The first time I heard *Take Me Out To The Ball Game*, it was being played by Dave Donohoe's Band in Peterborough, England - probably in about 1988. It must have struck me forcibly at the time; otherwise, how would I still remember the occasion?

Now I have come across the song on YouTube being played in New Orleans by *Loose Marbles*. These musicians play to the highest standards, virtually every day; and to them this was probably just another routine performance. But to the rest of us it is a most exhilarating example of how to play traditional jazz really well. You can view it here:

https://www.youtube.com/watch?v=BBHn3dtqjos

The tune romps along, supported by a driving rhythm section of Robin, John, Julie and Todd (the latter on guitar on this occasion). The melody is led in turn by Michael (clarinet), Barnabus (trombone) and Marla (trumpet). Note how brilliantly during the opening choruses these three support each other with the subtlest of quiet background colouring: for me, this is traditional jazz at its very best. And there is a terrific ensemble chorus at the end: you could say it's restrained or understated (nobody is over-blowing) and yet WOW! What excitement! Yes, the playing succeeds in being tasteful and yet thrilling throughout. Marla's vocal is delivered naturally, from the heart, without electronic amplification.

Many thanks to the video-maker codenamed *Wild Bill* for filming it.

Amazing to think *Take Me Out To The Ball Game* was written as long ago as 1908. The composer was Albert Von Tilzer. Lyrics were provided by Jack Norworth (*Take me out to the ball game.*

*Take me out with the crowd. Buy me some peanuts and crackerjack. I don't care if I never get back...*etc. As Marla sings it - no doubt thinking of her Toronto background! - *If the Blue Jays don't win it's a shame!*)

It was originally a waltz, complete with a 32-bar Verse; but for traditional jazz purposes it works brilliantly in 4/4 time if you play just the 32-bar Chorus [16 + 16 structure] in stomping fashion. Improvising is easy, involving some familiar four-bar blocks.

For those of us outside the USA, this is all very exciting; but my friend in Florida James Sterling tells me Americans still sing the tune all the time, especially at the ball games, and in the original waltz tempo.

'ALMOST AFRAID TO LOVE'

Tuba Skinny has given us a mind-boggling performance that serves as a lesson to us all. We have to thank the generous and prolific film-maker codenamed *digitalalexa* for making it available to us on YouTube. I am speaking about *Almost Afraid to Love*. It was composed by Ann Turner in 1938 and made famous at that time by the great blues singer Georgia White.

On the face of it, no performance could be simpler. It's just seven choruses of a 12-bar blues in C - 84 bars of music in all. But the way it is interpreted is exemplary - demonstrating all that is great about traditional jazz at its best:

Chorus 1: Against a solid foundation provided by the tuba, washboard, guitar and bass drum, the cornet introduces us to the tune; but the music is like a conversation between three old friends. Using her cup mute, Shaye makes the sad statements and Barnabus (trombone) and Ewan (clarinet) respond sympathetically to everything the cornet says.

Chorus 2: Erika begins to sing, telling the story with an uncluttered accompaniment. What a solid foundation Todd gives (as usual) on the tuba!

Chorus 3: Erika completes the story - with Shaye providing tasteful background colouring, using the cup mute.

Chorus 4: Ensemble. Both the cornet and trombone are muted now. This is another chorus sounding like a conversation between three old friends. It reminds me of the string quartets of Haydn and Mozart. Some of the phrases are exquisite - such as Shaye's phrase responding to the trombone at 1 min. 49secs. [I think this must be one of Shaye's favourite phrases - you hear it frequently in her playing.]

Chorus 5: The 'conversation' continues; with Ewan making assertive statements on his clarinet, while the cornet and trombone reply 'Yes, we know. It's a shame. You're so right!'

Chorus 6: Erika resumes the song.

Chorus 7: Erika completes the song, but with the others performing like the Greek Chorus from *Oedipus Rex* - commenting sympathetically on the events of the story. It is outstandingly good four-part interplay with the singer. And as the performance comes to an end, there's one more surprise in store. Shaye picks up her 'jam funnel' mute for a strong conclusive effect in the final two bars, descending a C minor arpeggio.

There is nothing strenuous or over-loud or showy or raucous about this performance. There are no screaming high notes. The playing gives the illusion of being totally relaxed, simple and effortless. But the apparent simplicity conceals art of the highest order.

Here's where to watch the performance:
https://www.youtube.com/watch?v=S12hvtvb0gU

A GREAT CD FROM THE SHOTGUN JAZZ BAND

Many people seem to have enjoyed the video I made of *The Shotgun Jazz Band* giving a pulsating performance of *Climax Rag*. I filmed it when I saw them at The Spotted Cat, New Orleans, in April 2015. If you would like to watch it, here's where to find it:

https://www.youtube.com/watch?v=h77s41Q0w5o

But may I also remind you that late in 2014 this great jazz band released a CD that is well worth listening to? It is packed with riches. If you would like to buy it, go to:

https://shotgunjazzband.bandcamp.com/album/yearning

and follow the instructions.

All sixteen tracks of the CD (entitled 'Yearning') were recorded in one session without an audience in the building that used to be Luthjens Dance Hall in New Orleans. For bands with less stamina, it would have been an exhausting undertaking. The acoustics are terrific but obviously the emptiness of the building meant that it lacked the atmosphere that comes from having an audience. The recording is well balanced: you hear all instruments and vocals clearly.

The Band on the day comprised Marla Dixon (trumpet), John Dixon (banjo), Tyler Thomson (string bass), Justin Peake (percussion), Ben Polcer (piano), Charlie Halloran (trombone) and James Evans (reeds).

As well as playing the trumpet in a bold, forthright manner, Marla also delivers lusty, emotional vocals, in which one of her specialities is the thrilling rising glissando.

The rock-steady rhythm section, which is responsible for much of the band's distinctive house style, is on superb form throughout. The combination of Justin Peake (one of my favourite drummers), Tyler Thomson and John Dixon would be hard to beat. What a joy it must be for horn players to be pumped along by them.

Here are the tunes on the CD:

<u>I Believe I Can Make It By Myself</u>

Sammy Penn with the Kid Thomas Band used to make a big feature of this 12-bar tune in Bb. The Shotgun Band gives it a raw treatment, with much trumpet growling and flattened thirds as well as a lusty vocal from Marla.

<u>You Always Hurt The One You Love</u>

This sets a great foot-tapping tempo. The rhythm section shines. Note the unusual key change - after a start in Bb, Marla sings the vocal gently in Eb and later more powerfully in Bb.

<u>Get A Working Man</u> (a.k.a. *Pinchbacks, Take 'Em Away*)

Marla offers a vocal with a message for the ladies: it's better to have a hard-working man than one who is good-looking but idle. It was originally recorded in 1924 by Bessie Smith under the title *Pinchbacks, Take 'Em Away*. It has a 16-bar verse and a 32-bar chorus (harmonically identical to *It's a Long Way to Tipperary*). James' fluid solo (backed so well by Charlie and the Rhythm Section) distinctly demonstrates the Shotgun house style.

<u>Tears</u>

This raggy number which I think Lil Hardin composed for King Oliver's Band in 1923 (when they recorded it) is technically challenging but the Shotguns make light work of it. The tune is played fast (as by King Oliver) and, although it's full ensemble all the way, there are some nice 'breaks' for James.

Dream

Marla delivers a pleasant vocal (complete with Verse) right from the start, with solid backing from Ben, John, Tyler and Justin. Then there's a relaxed chorus featuring the clarinet and trombone again, with the chosen key (F) suited very well to James' higher register.

Yearning

This standard from 1925 seems to be a favourite with the Shotgun players. They played it in the great Abita Springs video. Marla offers a punchy trumpet and vocal and there is a pleasant 16-bars-each chorus shared by James and Charlie.

Hindustan

Every band plays this tune from 1918. So how do the Shotguns make it fresh? With terrific interplay; some Kid Thomas-style attack; and a vocal from Marla.

He'll Have To Go

This is one of two tunes in waltz time on the CD. Imagine *Careless Love* played slowly in 3/4. It's harmonically similar. Composed by Joe and Audrey Allison, it was a hit for Jim Reeves in 1959. Much of the performance consists of a gentle vocal from Marla, well supported by Ben. There are a few bars of special beauty when James leads with the melody in the ensemble.

Over In The Gloryland

This spiritual is another tune that most bands play. Some musicians don't like it because of its very limited harmonic pattern. But the Shotguns make it last for over six minutes and leave you wanting more. There is hearty singing and great collective improvisation.

I Love You So Much It Hurts

This is a country and western number recorded (and probably written) by Floyd Tillman in 1948. The Shotguns give a no-frills straight-ahead performance of the 32-bar simple tune. They choose not to offer a vocal.

Kentucky Blues

I don't know the origin of this tune. (There are at least two other different tunes with this title). It seems to have two themes (16-bar and a standard 12-bar). The arrangement is the most sophisticated on this CD - from a band that normally does not bother with very sophisticated arrangements. The lovely clarinet of James Evans is well featured.

Love In Bloom

James is no mean vocalist. It's a lovely song composed in 1934 by Leo Robin and Ralph Rainger. James also plays some fluid clarinet with Marla (for once using a standard mute) in the background. It's one of two tunes played in Ab. The other is *Gloryland*, of course.

Mobile Stomp

This famous number (written and recorded by the Sam Morgan Band in 1927) is also on the Abita Springs video. I like the rock-steady work from all members of the band, especially at its more delicate moments. Note the saxophone's second chorus against offbeats; and the amusing 'quadruple' ending.

You Broke Your Promise

This 1949 pop song by Wyle, Taylor and Pole was a favourite with the early Preservation Hall bands. In an unpretentious performance of this 32-bar tune, Marla offers a nice clear vocal - a help to those of us who want to learn the words. As in *You Always Hurt The One You Love*, above, she drops the key (to C) for her first vocal but sings her second vocal higher - in F - the key in which the rest of the performance is played. This must be a device she enjoys. It certainly is effective in setting the two vocals in contrast.

Tennessee Waltz

This is the second tune in 3/4 time. It's also the most touching tune on the CD. Marla sings the sad words about lost love, with good instrumental support from James and Charlie. A beautiful melody, gently presented.

I'll See You In My Dreams

The famous Isham Jones and Sammy Kahn song from 1924. No vocal is offered; and they do not make the mistake of taking it too slowly. Charlie's trombone gives a melodious lead; and there is some tender ensemble playing.

AND AN ALBUM IN 2017!

On New Year's Day 2017, Marla and John Dixon's *Shotgun Jazz Band* released their latest Album, entitled *Stepping On The Gas*.

It was recorded, like their previous one, at the former Luthjens' Dance Hall. The acoustics were again terrific. Every instrument can be clearly heard. Basically, a six-piece band was used. This was the regular five - Marla Dixon on vocals and trumpet, John Dixon on banjo, James Evans (reeds), Charlie Halloran (trombone) and Tyler Thomson on string bass - plus David Boeddinghaus on piano. But on six tracks they became a 'Big Band' by adding Ben Polcer on trumpet and Tom Fischer on reeds.

The combination of John Dixon on banjo and Tyler Thomson on string bass is just about the greatest in the world for driving along the raw style of New Orleans jazz in rock-steady four-to-the-bar form, and they are well complemented here by the totally dependable David Boeddinghaus. As for James Evans, he is now established as one of the greatest reed-players to be heard anywhere. He has that wonderful artist's knack of making everything sound relaxed, even though he always plays in a hugely creative and technically brilliant manner. And fans of the trombonist Charlie Halloran will particularly enjoy his lusty contributions on such numbers as *Smiles*, *My Old Kentucky Home*, *She's Crying for Me*, and *Old Miss Rag*. He adds so much to the gutsy, gritty qualities of which the band is proud. Marla, of course, is a gem - great as a band-leader, one of the best trumpet-players and always passionate and distinctive in her singing. She seems to me to know virtually every tune in the book and to have memorised the words of hundreds of songs.

This recording is specially exciting because, in terms of personnel, width of repertoire and quality of the arrangements, it is the most ambitious album the band has made.

I often complain that bands spin out tunes for seven or eight minutes, even when nobody is dancing. They seem to think almost every member of the band *must* solo on at least one 32-bar chorus. Such performances can be so dreary. It would be better to keep tunes brief (as they were on the great recordings of the 1920s).

On this album, *The Shotgun Jazz Band* seems to have adopted exactly that philosophy. Eight of the tunes are completed in under three minutes. And only three tracks run for over four minutes. This also allows for a goodly number and variety of tunes on the Album: there are 18 in all.

As the title suggests, much of the Album is inspired by the work of the Sam Morgan band, whose recording of *Stepping on the Gas* (1927) is closely imitated by the *Shotgun*, right through to the neat Coda. The Sam Morgan band used two reeds and two trumpets. I guess that is why the Dixons added the extra two instruments for this track. Their 'Big Band' is used to good effect on this tune, as well as on *She's Crying for Me*, *Down by the Riverside* and *Old Miss Rag*.

Throughout the album, notice the use of neat, intelligent head arrangements usually showing great respect for the original recordings. For example, *White Ghost Shivers* (for me the most interesting track) closely follows the original recording made in the 1920s by *The New Orleans Owls*. It is a romping number which, to my ear, appears to begin with a spooky theme in C minor, followed by a 16-bar theme in E flat and a further 16-bar theme in A flat – both the latter allowing for plenty of little breaks. There is a great Coda, just as on the original 1920s recording.

She's Crying for Me - also played by the 'Big Band' - is similarly close to the original 1925 *New Orleans Rhythm Kings* version composed by Santo Pecora. Essentially in A flat, it is complete with the two key changes taking it into and then out of F for a 12-bar blues interlude.

With some of the tunes, you feel immediately as if you were at The Spotted Cat in New Orleans, with Marla's regular band of five or six musicians in cracking form. This is especially true of *Smiles*, *The Curse of An Aching Heart*, *Pretend*, *Whenever Your Lonesome*, and *My Old Kentucky Home*. On this last number, Tyler is the singer: it has become one of his party pieces.

There are some interesting performances of obscure numbers. For example, *Rose of Bombay* is a tune I had not heard before. Apparently it was recorded in 1923 on an Edison Cylinder by *Rudy Wiedoeft's Californians*. It is a pleasant leisurely number with a Verse followed by a 32-bar Chorus somewhat reminiscent of *Hindustan*: it uses plenty of minims and semi-breves.

Then there is *Guilty* – not the song of that name recorded in the 1930s by such singers as Billie Holiday and Al Bowlly - but rather one written and recorded in 1974 by Randy Newman. Marla sings it, accompanied by John on the banjo for a whole two minutes before the full band joins in.

In *Breeze* and *Moonlight Bay* the band plays the Verses as well as the Choruses! I bet there were not many of us who knew these Verses.

Marla also sings *I Hate a Man Like You*; and the entire album begins in a surprisingly simple, tasteful way with *Gulf Coast Blues*, the 1923 composition by Clarence Williams, recorded by Bessie Smith, which Marla sings mostly with accompaniment by David on piano - very much on the lines of the original, with David taking the Clarence Williams rôle.

Another interesting vocal is *How Am I To Know?*, sung by James Evans. Apparently it comes from a 1920s film called 'Dynamite' and was composed by Jack King with lyrics by Dorothy Parker, no less!

The old pop tune *Pretend You're Happy When You're Blue*, composed by Lew Douglas, Cliff Parman, Frank LaVere and Dan Belloc, is very pleasantly performed, with a vocal from Marla. Why did it take so many people to compose it?! (I believe it was actually Lew Douglas who did most of the work.) After the final vocal, the *Shotgun* round it off (as also in *My Old Kentucky Home*) from the Middle Eight - a tactic we should all adopt from time to time.

Charlie takes the lead very movingly on the oldest composition on the Album - *Deep River*, which is the final track and very effectively winds down the concert. What a beautiful way to bring the Album to an end!

But now you need to know how to obtain the Album. The simplest way is on line. I found that it downloads in less than half a minute. The wonders of technology! Here's where to go:

https://shotgunjazzband.bandcamp.com/

VIDEO MAKERS

I feel so privileged to have lived to an age when - at my computer here in Nottingham - I am able to click a button and watch wonderful traditional jazz performances from all around the world.

We have to be deeply grateful to all the generous and hard-working video-makers who provide us with these treats. Some of them have super equipment. They use two or more cameras and have a separate sound-recording apparatus.

But when I decided to have a go at making some videos, I bought a simple Panasonic Lumix camera. It is intended for taking still photographs but, like most cameras these days, it has a built-in microphone and the facility to record videos. It also has a useful 'zoom' feature.

Once you have made a video, it is easy to load it on to such a site as YouTube, thereby making it available to viewers all over the world. You have merely to follow the simple instructions on the screen.

So far, I have had only four or five opportunities to film really great jazz bands. But I have made a number of videos and put them on YouTube. My favourite - the one of which I am most proud - shows *The Shotgun Jazz Band* at The Spotted Cat Club (New Orleans) playing *Royal Garden Blues* when I was there for the French Quarter Festival in April 2015. The band was on absolutely cracking form and I was able to film from the side, very near the band, so I obtained some pleasing close-up shots of Haruka, Marla, James, John and Tyler. If you have not yet seen that video, you can watch it here:

https://www.youtube.com/watch?v=Dv5RBMA_v4k

And if, like me, you spend many hours watching YouTube videos of traditional jazz bands playing in the USA - and particularly in New Orleans, you must have noticed that dozens of them have been put up by two enthusiasts who use the code-names *digitalalexa* and *RaoulDuke504*. We owe them a huge debt of gratitude; and I think the bands too must be grateful to these people for spreading their fame to many thousands throughout the world.

A great experience I had in New Orleans during April 2015 was meeting these video-makers for the first time. They were enthusiastically filming at the French Quarter Festival.

RaoulDuke504, who works as a chef, has the advantage of living only fifty miles from New Orleans. I had the great privilege of shaking his hand and thanking him for the pleasure he has given me (and so many thousands of people) with his wonderful videos.

Digitalalexa is actually two people - husband Al and his wife Judy from New Jersey. They have travelled down frequently to New Orleans and had a grand time filming their favourite bands. Al and Judy film the same performance from different angles and when they return home Al edits the two videos into one, trying to make the most of the best shots they have obtained between them. It was a great honour to meet Al and Judy several times at various events. Al told me his videos by 2015 had over three million hits.

These wonderful modest people enjoy their relative anonymity. But I must say a Big Thank You to them for bringing us so much pleasure.

SECTION 2: THINKING ABOUT THE MUSIC

Now I want to offer you some observations and opinions and pass on some of the discoveries that have brought me pleasure over recent years.

THE STATE OF TRADITIONAL JAZZ TODAY

Is our music dying out? The answer is 'NO!'

There are plenty of wonderful young musicians around the globe who have discovered the musical styles and repertoire of a century ago and are playing traditional jazz with great skill and passion. For an immediate example, have a look at a video of *Over the Waves,* played by young musicians in Tokyo to see what I mean:

https://www.youtube.com/watch?v=KBuXLwcnvvg

But let me tell you about what has happened here in England. Back in the 1950s and 1960s, traditional jazz was extremely popular in Britain. There were hundreds of bands, from full-time professionals performing at the Royal Festival Hall to enthusiastic amateurs who entertained in the back rooms of pubs. Their music was inspired by the New Orleans and Chicago jazz of the period 1910 - 1930 and also by the revival of traditional jazz after the Second World War by bands such as that of George Lewis. Occasionally a record made by a British jazz band would even make it into the week's 'Top Ten'. But from the era of the Beatles and disco music onwards, traditional jazz fell into decline. It is now given very little air time on British radio and virtually none on television.

Ten years ago, I noticed audiences at traditional jazz club concerts in England were becoming sparse and the average age of members of the bands was about 65.

Now, it's even worse: there are places where you can find trad jazz being played in Britain (usually still in the back rooms of pubs) but the musicians are dying out. A typical pub band today comprises musicians aged 75 or over.

But I constantly hear of new young bands setting up, especially elsewhere in the world. One of the latest is *The Stone Arch Jazz Band* in Minneapolis, founded by the talented and tasteful clarinet-player Richard Lund. Have a look at their website. And note that the band has already made some stylish videos.

And in Chicago a band called *The Fat Babies* plays regularly. I know this band is highly respected by fellow musicians. You can find many examples of their work on YouTube.

And *The Dirty River Dixie Band*, founded in Texas and playing a very energetic kind of dixieland music, was able to announce towards the end of 2016 that the average age of its members was under 25.

The situation in such countries as Australia, Germany, Canada, Spain, Italy and Denmark, as far as I can tell, gives some encouragement. Ray Andrew in Perth, Australia, told me the traditional jazz scene is very strong in his city and that the young are being attracted to it. And Michael Meissner introduced me to *Queen Porter Stomp* in Sydney. You can easily find examples of this young band's work on YouTube.

Dutch jazzman Robert Duis recommended looking at videos of *Malo's Hot Five* and *Attila's Rollini Project*; and my friend Anders Winnberg in Sweden has assured me there are plenty of good bands operating in his country, where the Gothenburg Jazz Festival is a major event. Even Finland - a country remote from New Orleans and with a population of well under six million - has the very pleasant *Birger's Ragtime Band*. Also in Finland there is a band called *Doctor Jazz*: it seems to me to be bright and recently formed; and several of the players are relatively young.

Friend Phil in the USA recommended to me the Moscow-based young bands *The Kickipickles* and *The Moscow Ragtime*

Band. You can also sample them on YouTube. And in Japan, especially, as I indicated, traditional jazz seems to be going through a boom period. Some of the best in the world is being played in Tokyo.

Above all, I can tell you there is great old-time jazz being played by YOUNG people on the streets of New Orleans. They are the hope for the future; and I believe the Internet is spreading their influence so rapidly that there will be yet another big revival of this kind of music.

In the days before Hurricane Katrina, you would have thought of Bourbon Street as the main hub for jazz in New Orleans. But now it is Frenchmen Street, in the Faubourg Marigny - a road full of jazz bars and clubs. There are over twenty traditional jazz bands playing professionally in New Orleans - more than at any previous time in jazz history.

To see what I mean, even if you can't get to New Orleans, try investigating the scene there on YouTube. You will be amazed at the quality of the traditional jazz being produced by instrumentalists in their twenties and thirties; and there are plenty of singers of outstanding ability too.

Tuba Skinny is currently considered the best of all the groups. They are not only technically brilliant; they also take great care over arrangements and presentation of tunes, and they have been reviving good old melodies that were in danger of being forgotten. Have a look and listen to their work. But you may also care to try any of these groups on YouTube. Just type their names in and indulge yourself with some fine music:

Tuba Skinny

Rhythm Wizards Jazz Band Sample their tasteful playing at: https://www.youtube.com/watch?v=ZK8rhXX2rpk

Loose Marbles

Little Big Horns

The Cottonmouth Kings

Smoking Time Jazz Band

Jessy Carolina and the Hot Mess

Jenavieve Cook and the Royal Street Winding Boys

Yes Ma'am String Band

The Shotgun Jazz Band (led by the dynamic Canadian trumpeter and singer Marla Dixon) For an exciting example of this band's work, look at this video that I personally filmed: https://www.youtube.com/watch?v=Dv5RBMA_v4k

Stalebread Scottie and His Gang

The Gentilly Stompers

Emily Estrella and the Faux Barrio Billionaires (Emily is originally from Cincinnati)

Hokum High Rollers

The Sluetown Strutters

The Palmetto Bug Stompers

The Jazz Vipers

The New Orleans Swamp Donkeys

Orleans 6 (led by the excellent Ben Polcer)

Sour Mash Hug Band

Baby Soda

In St. Louis, Missouri, *The Sidney Street Shakers* play exactly the kind of jazz I like best - unpretentious, straightforward, exciting, with good teamwork and just right for dancers. And note elsewhere *The California Feet Warmers* - a fairly young band playing slick, well-prepared traditional jazz.

All terrific stuff. So heart-warming; and giving great hope for the future.

And even in Britain there is hope. Have a look at the videos of *The Brownfield/Byrne Hot Six* to discover some technically-brilliant swinging jazz being played by chaps still in their twenties and thirties. Also from Britain, seek out the videos of Adrian Cox, or Ben Cummings, or The Graham Hughes Sunshine Kings, or Giacomo Smith, or *The Basin Street Brawlers*. You will have a pleasant surprise.

Elsewhere, you may find such good young bands as *Magic Shook Heads* and *The Hippocampus Jass Gang* in the south of France: their videos are worth watching. And in Buenos Aires, you have the *Jazz Friends* - a terrific, fluent band, whose range of instruments sometimes includes the 'pinkullo' - a South American flute.

In the North-Eastern corner of Italy we find the young *Adovabadan Jazz Band* of Treviso playing some very tasteful traditional jazz. You can see them performing *Cake Walking Babies From Home* on this YouTube video:

https://www.youtube.com/watch?v=5aGsU4qG624

In the Rhine-Neckar area of Germany, a newly-formed band of energetic and enthusiastic young musicians has shown what can be achieved even with a limited range of instruments. They call themselves *Die Selbsthilfe-Gruppe* (*The Self-Help Group*) and you can find examples of their work on YouTube.

WHAT IS TRADITIONAL JAZZ?

Recently I was present when two friends - both jazz musicians - got into an argument about what exactly traditional jazz is. One of them took the 'purist' line that traditional jazz is what was played in New Orleans by *black* musicians in the first three decades of the Twentieth Century. Only those black musicians, he said, could really feel the music and instinctively play the blues scales. He said that later traditional jazz, largely played by white musicians, should just be called 'Dixieland' - music that was slick and often polished but lacking in the true blues feeling.

It reminded me of the arguments on the same topic that my schoolboy friends John, Ian and Derek used to have in the 1950s, when the British trad jazz boom began. We called the music 'trad'; but John and Derek said British bands were producing only a commercialised, sanitised copy of authentic New Orleans traditional jazz. (I kept out of these arguments. I just wished I could play it - sanitised or not!)

Well, I am not going to attempt a dictionary-style definition of traditional jazz. But I will tell you what the music encompasses – for me, at least. I include *all* the following terms and probably more.

'Trad'
New Orleans Jazz
Dixieland
Ragtime
Chicago-Style Jazz
West Coast Jazz
Jug and String-Band Music

For me traditional jazz is about a style of playing: a group of musicians take a tune and agree the key, the melody and the chord sequence and away they go, playing the material and improvising around it. Generally there is a fixed tempo and generally the 'choruses' are repeated end-to-end as many times as required. There may or may not be an agreed musical arrangement - either a 'head' arrangement or one on paper. The tunes are drawn largely but not exclusively from the repertoires of the classic jazz bands from the first half of the Twentieth Century and from popular music generally.

Nor do I have a fixed idea about what instruments a traditional jazz band should contain. I think traditional jazz can be played by any number of players - from one to perhaps as many as ten (provided they do not tread on each other's toes).

I do not even believe that a band should comprise a 'front line' of trumpet, clarinet and trombone and a 'rhythm section' of bass (tuba or string), drums and chord instrument (guitar, banjo or piano). Although this concept has worked well for many bands for decades, I think traditional jazz being played by bands that include a violin, a washboard, a harmonica or whatever is just as valid. Look at photos from the bands of the 1920s: there are various combinations of instruments and you often find the leader was a violinist.

What I do not count as traditional jazz is 'free jazz'. And 'modern jazz' is not quite traditional jazz either, though there is more overlap with traditional jazz than some think.

Do the musicians have to be black in order to achieve greatness? Well, certainly when you listen to such a player as Johnny Dodds, you understand why some theorists think so. But white musicians have contributed massively to the history of traditional jazz, in composing and performing. And now we have the new generation of young musicians who have gravitated to the streets of New Orleans. Most of them are white; and they play with great technique and feeling. *Their* music - for me - is traditional jazz.

I was at a traditional jazz concert recently when a lady in the audience said she was enjoying it very much but, she said, 'I don't normally listen to such erudite music'.

I was struck by the word 'erudite', partly because it's not a word you often hear, but even more because it was a word I had never myself applied to traditional jazz.

However, when I reflected on it afterwards, I came to see that it really was a clever choice of word and very appropriate to our music.

If we think of traditional jazz only as a pleasant noise that makes us tap our feet and want to dance, we are missing the enormous amount of learning that lies behind it. And the greatest musicians make it look so easy that we may not recognise how 'erudite' it is.

The Merriam-Webster Dictionary defines 'erudite' as 'having or showing knowledge that is gained by studying'. The Concise Oxford Dictionary tells us that 'erudite' means 'remarkably learned'.

When you think about it, you find a huge amount of erudition behind every performance of traditional jazz.

The musicians had to:

1. master the techniques of playing their instrument(s) [many hundreds of hours of practice];

2. study the history of traditional jazz and learn from the work and recordings of past masters;

3. learn to play in various keys and become fluent in the appropriate chords and arpeggios - major, minor, diminished and so on - and be able to improvise freely around them;

4. study and learn to use syncopation, riffs, jazzy devices and a variety of tempos and rhythms;

5. understand the structures of the tunes;

6. learn and hold in their heads the melodies and harmonic progressions of many tunes [often hundreds];

7. study the role of their own instrument and use this knowledge effectively in contributing to the playing as a team-member;

8. master the conventions and the methods of communication within a performance.

Compared with most conventional kinds of musicians who play instruments directly from printed music and without any requirement to improvise or deviate from what is written, jazz musicians may be considered *exceptionally* erudite.

Imagine you would like to speak a foreign language but you are starting from scratch. Think how much study it will take for you to reach a point when you will be able to hold a fluent natural conversation with native speakers of that language.

Learning to play an instrument in a traditional jazz band is very similar to that.

Yes, well said that lady: traditional jazz is erudite all right.

RECOMMENDED – JAZZ WITH LUNCH

Many traditional jazz fans are elderly people who have the time and appetite (in all senses) to go out for some music, a drink and a meal at lunchtime. Many of them have told me they much prefer this to going to jazz clubs in the evenings. They say they do not like to be out late at night, especially if there is a tricky journey home. And, of course, admission is free at these pub lunchtime concerts.

Also, most members of our bands are themselves elderly and no longer have day jobs, so they too are available to play at lunchtime. What could be better for them than to go and give some entertainment, keeping in practice and sharing their joy in the music? In addition, there's always a good chance of getting younger people interested - those who casually pop into the pub for a drink and are pleasantly surprised by what they hear.

I am speaking of course of the situation here in England but I guess the same is true in many other countries.

I'm pleased to report that the message is getting across here in the English Midlands. I know of six pubs providing lunchtime jazz within a few miles of my home.

Let me give you the story behind a successful example.

In the beginning, there was a defunct building (*The Coronation Hotel*) for sale in Baker Street, Alvaston. This is on the south-eastern edge of the great city of Derby.

The hotel was acquired in 2015 by The Steamin' Billy Brewing Co. Ltd., which then renamed it simply as *The Coronation* and carried out an extensive refurbishment.

It has a decent-sized car park. Excellent meals and drinks are available at reasonable prices. The stone-baked pizzas are a speciality.

Best news of all, though, is that the management strongly supports traditional jazz. They invited Dave Harmer (the popular trombonist and manager of Leicester's *New Orleans Hot Shots*) to bring along some of his friends every Wednesday lunchtime to play for the diners.

So, starting on Wednesday, 9 December 2015, Dave provided a quartet.

And there has been traditional jazz from 12.30pm until 2.45pm at *The Coronation* every Wednesday since then. Word soon got round and the audience has grown to a very good size, with many 'regulars'.

More good news is that yet another pub in the English Midlands started in May 2016 to have traditional jazz in the lunchtimes. The pub is *The Boathouse* at *Barrow-on-Soar* (beautifully situated on the river bank between Loughborough and Leicester). *The Secret Jazz Band* was booked to play every second and fourth Monday of the month, between 12.30pm and 2.30pm. The band gave its first performance on 9 May 2016, when there was some fine music and a good audience enjoying the sunshine at the tables overlooking the river. Some of the boating people moored up and stopped to have a lunch and hear the jazz, too.

The Secret Jazz Band was formed in June 2014. The percussionist Alan Cole had been invited to provide a six-piece traditional jazz band for a once-a-month Thursday lunchtime session at another public house - *The Dog and Gun* in Syston, Leicester. He agreed to do this - and then set about forming a band.

Alan gave the band the working title of *The Secret Jazz Band* (secret because he did not know who the musicians would be) – and the name has stuck.

Alan did not have much difficulty in finding players who said they would be happy to spend a lunchtime, at least occasionally, taking part in a relaxed jam session. They knew it would provide a good opportunity to have fun and keep in practice.

Since then, *The Secret Jazz Band* has played every month at *The Dog and Gun*. It is a pub that looks after its customers well, and offers a good lunch.

The band does not get together to rehearse, so it generally sticks to familiar, uncomplicated numbers – such as *Make Me A Pallet on the Floor*, *Running Wild*, *Alexander's Ragtime Band*, *When You're Smiling*, *The Girls Go Crazy*, *Hindustan*, *Careless Love*.

The audience grew over the months and reached 45 when I was last there, so the bar was crowded.

If a pub manager can make some kind of offer, such as a free drink for the band and a small donation towards their expenses, a tips jar can also be passed round among the audience, who, if they wish, may contribute a coin or two. In this way, the musicians should at least cover their travelling expenses. That is how the system successfully operates at the pubs where I have been present at such performances in recent weeks.

I know of six pubs in Nottinghamshire, Derbyhire, and Leicestershire where I can confirm the music is being regularly offered at least once a month at lunchtimes at the time of writing.

WHAT ARE 'BLUES'?

A friend asked me to explain the type-names we come across in traditional jazz tune titles. 'What is the difference between a *Drag* and a *Rag*?' he asked. 'What exactly is a *Stomp*? How do you define *Blues*?'

Little did he know I am just as confused about these matters as he is. There is plenty to read on the subjects, both in books and on the internet; but agreed definitions are not easy to come by.

Worst of all is trying to define *Blues*. In the 1940s, the first 'Blues' I became aware of were the songs of Bessie Smith and her contemporaries. There were tunes such as *Backwater Blues* and *Blue Spirit Blues*. I was led to believe the Blues were mournful songs, expressing suffering or regrets, or at least wistfulness and nostalgia. The books I read suggested they had arisen from the chanting of African slaves and were structured on a familiar twelve-bar chord pattern (three four-bar blocks). They used a scale in which flattened thirds, fifths and sevenths were common.

But just think of the heritage of tunes with 'Blues' in the title today.

There are songs called 'Blues' that are really just run-of-the-mill pop music of ninety years ago (normally 32-bar structures). Think of *Beer Garden Blues* (a conventional 32 bars in AABA structure). Think of *Tishomingo Blues*, *Sugar Blues* (this one actually an 18-bar, including tag), *Bye Bye Blues*, *Wild Man Blues*, *Rent Party Blues*, and *Davenport Blues*.

When professional composers got to work on writing 'Blues', their inventiveness took them far beyond creating one mournful melody of 12 bars. You find *Yellow Dog Blues*, *Savoy*

Blues, Riverside Blues, Perdido Street Blues, Royal Garden Blues, Jackass Blues, Aunt Hagar's Blues, Dippermouth Blues, Livery Stables Blues, Beale Street Blues, Canal Street Blues, St. Louis Blues, West End Blues, Tin Roof Blues, Chimes Blues - all having two or more (often very cheerful) 12-bar themes and in some cases further structuring, such as 'bridge' passages and key changes.

The early classic *Crazy Blues* has a long, continuous vocal that runs through three themes. Only the middle one comprises 12 bars; but you would hardly be aware of it.

There are tunes with a 12-bar theme but also a substantial and memorable verse that is played before it. Think of *Memphis Blues*.

There are plenty of 'Blues' that are lovely wistful compositions that do not include a 12-bar theme at all - *Basin Street Blues, Melancholy Blues, Wabash Blues, Michigander Blues, Owl Call Blues, Winin' Boy Blues, Faraway Blues*, for example.

Some tunes called 'Blues' have no 12-bar theme and nothing 'bluesy' about them, but are simply well-structured fun numbers. Think of *Wolverine Blues, Blue Grass Blues, Dangerous Blues* and *Jazz Me Blues*.

Sometimes the 12-bar blues structure turns up in unlikely places. For example, *Mahogany Hall Stomp* (yes - it's called a stomp) has a simple main second theme of 12 bars on which the musicians improvise. The same thing happens in *She's Crying For Me, Copenhagen*, and especially in *The Chant*, which sounds like a very tricky piece, even though there is a simple 12-bar section tucked away within it as a basis for improvisations.

And what about *Tom Cat Blues*? It actually sounds like the 12-bar song *Nobody Knows The Way I Feel This Morning* leading (usually with a change of key) into the 16-bar *Winin' Boy Blues*.

And consider *Weary Blues*. Band-leaders often tell you it is not a blues and it is certainly not weary. In fact the first two themes are 12-bar structures, though they whip along in such a way that you would hardly notice. Then, with a change of key, you are into the pulsating familiar 16-bar theme on which sparkling improvisations are possible.

So: what kind of tune may legitimately be called a 'Blues'? I have no idea.

WHY ARE HYMNS AND SPIRITUALS IN OUR REPERTOIRE?

We take it for granted that hymns and spirituals have a place in our repertoires. But they still occasionally take people by surprise. For example, some weeks ago, friends and I were playing in Oakham, a market town in Central England. One of our tunes was *The Old Rugged Cross*. An elderly gentleman told us how much he had enjoyed it. He said he had never realised that a hymn could work well when played by a jazz band.

You hardly ever hear a traditional jazz concert in which there is not at least one hymn or spiritual. Also, audiences no longer feel uncomfortable (as English people would have done a hundred years ago) about dancing to such religious music.

Among the most popular titles are:

At The Cross
Down By the Riverside
Does Jesus Care?
Sing On
God Will Take Care Of You
On Higher Ground
Only a Look
Over in the Gloryland
Satan, Your Kingdom Must Come Down
Royal Telephone
His Eye is on the Sparrow
In the Sweet By and By
The Old Rugged Cross
What a Friend We Have in Jesus
Just a Closer Walk With Thee

Take My Hand, Precious Lord
We Shall Walk Through the Streets of the City
Where He Leads Me
It is No Secret
The Lily of the Valley
The Saints Go Marching In

I began to wonder how it came about that such tunes have a place alongside the old pop songs, blues and rags in our repertoire.

It's easy to believe the myth that spirituals were sung in the cotton fields by toiling slaves in the mid-Nineteenth Century and that - when jazz bands came into being - they would have played them and from about 1910 would have 'jazzed them up'.

But I'm not sure it's that simple. I have found no evidence that this happened. I can't find any recordings of spirituals or hymns by jazz bands before 1927. I think there's nothing in the early recordings of the ODJB, King Oliver, Kid Ory and so on.

So I prefer the following explanation.

In 1927, Columbia Records twice recorded the great Sam Morgan Band in New Orleans. The recordings were made in the Godchaux Building, 527, Canal Street. Four tunes were recorded on each occasion. The resulting eight recordings are still considered a hugely important part of the history of traditional jazz and have influenced hundreds of bands over the decades. The legend is that - like other jazz bands - the Sam Morgan Band played mostly for dancing and did not include religious music in its dance hall repertoire. However, one of the recording engineers was very keen on such tunes as *Down By The Riverside* and suggested that Sam's band should record them.

So the Band included three 'spirituals' in the eight recordings - and the rest is history: if Sam could do it, why not the rest of us?

Apparently trumpet-player Isaiah Morgan (Sam's brother) in a later interview made the point that jazz bands such as theirs might have played hymns and spirituals at funerals but would not have used religious music for dancing.

By 1940, it became commonplace for the most influential traditional jazz musicians to record spirituals. Think of George Lewis, Bunk Johnson, Louis Armstrong.

Quite a few spirituals we play - including some in my list above - were composed not in the days of slavery but in the days when jazz bands were already well established.

Here's a stirring modern example of a spiritual in a jazz band performance. In this video, we see two of the best bands in the world joining together to perform *Over in the Gloryland* - one of those spirituals made famous in 1927 by Sam Morgan:

https://www.youtube.com/watch?v=EAH7RhCNFko

JUDGING THE BAND

How do you judge the quality of the bands you listen to?

All assessments are subjective. Different people are impressed by different qualities. I remember a lady who used to judge bands almost entirely on the nattiness of their waistcoats!

However, I thought it might be interesting - and a bit of fun - to produce a check-list with a view to awarding marks for various aspects of a performance.

Give a mark out of ten to the band for each of the following. That gives a total maximum of 60.

1. Teamwork
2. Technical Ability
3. Interpretation of the tunes
4. Rapport with the Audience
5. On-Stage Behaviour and Presentation
6. Overall Good Value

What do you think of it? I tried applying it to ten bands I know well and the results range from 28 to 47 marks out of 60.

Although any of us can carry out such 'assessments', just for our own amusement, I think it would be a good idea for bands to conduct similar assessments of their own performances. It would indicate some of the areas they could work on in order to improve.

By the way, do you think there is any band capable of scoring the Maximum 60 points? I would of course nominate *The Shotgun Jazz Band*, based in New Orleans.

RECORDING JAZZ IN THE EARLY DAYS

What a performance it was, recording music in the early days - round about 1920, for example.

The sound had to be picked up through a funnel and - to achieve some kind of balance - the musicians had to be disposed at various distances from it. The vocalist, if any, would sing straight into the funnel.

On a related subject, here's a video you may find interesting. It shows Andy Schumm and fellow musicians, with the recording expertise of Shawn Borri, in 2012 recreating the wax cylinder recording techniques of about 100 years earlier:

https://www.youtube.com/watch?v=y3Wjv6K0c-4

At the end of the video, you get to hear the playback. Amazing!

ABUNDANCE OF TUNES IN THE EARLY DAYS

Historians have given many reasons why jazz developed in New Orleans when it did. There were so many influences and so many sources of inspiration.

But one reason that is often overlooked is that there were so many *tunes* available at the time that lent themselves conveniently to interpretation in a 'jazzy' way. I sometimes wonder whether early jazz would have developed without the abundance of suitable popular music at the time.

It was the age when you made your own musical entertainment in the home or you went to the music halls to find it. The early jazz bands had hundreds of tunes to choose from. Most have been long forgotten but just think about this: you could still today make up a good traditional jazz programme entirely from well-known tunes written more than 100 years ago.

Already by the early 1900s, such songs as these were available to the bands:

Beautiful Dreamer
After the Ball
You've Been a Good Old Wagon But You Done Broke Down
A Hot Time in Old Town
Way Down Upon the Swanee River
Ciribiribin
Smoky Mokes
Whistling Rufus
At a Georgia Camp Meeting
Maple Leaf Rag
My Wild Irish Rose

You Tell Me Your Dream

Creole Belle

Hiawatha

High Society

Indiana

Bill Bailey

The Entertainer

In the Sweet Bye and Bye

Oh Didn't He Ramble

Under the Bamboo Tree

Ida, Sweet as Apple Cider

Meet Me In St. Louis

And in the next ten years these were among the hundreds composed:

My Gal Sal

In the Shade of the Old Apple Tree

Redwing

Down in Jungle Town

Dusty Rag

Shine on Harvest Moon

Ace in the Hole

Meet Me Tonight in Dreamland

Put on Your Old Grey Bonnet

That's a Plenty

I Wonder Who's Kissing Her Now

Chinatown

Down By the Old Mill Stream

Some of these days

Silver Bell

Washington and Lee Swing

I Want a Girl Just like the Girl
Alexander's Ragtime Band
Oh You Beautiful Doll
Ballin' The Jack
Curse of an Aching Heart
You Made Me Love You
Down Among The Sheltering Palms
If I Had You
St Louis Blues
Twelfth Street Rag
When You Wore a Tulip
Yellow Dog Blues
Blame it on the Blues
Georgia Grind
Hesitating Blues
Memories
Paper Doll
When I Leave the World Behind

No wonder those early players - Buddy Bolden, Kid Ory and the like - could put on an entertaining programme for dancers. Such a thing would not be possible with the pop music of today. Not much of it lends itself readily to traditional jazz treatment.

SECTION 3: THE BANDS AND MUSICIANS

There are hundreds of great bands playing this music all over the world. No doubt you have your own local favourites. But I am going to offer you a very personal selection. I will tell you about bands and particular players I have discovered in recent years and enjoyed very much.

THE LOOSE MARBLES

I believe the most important traditional jazz band so far in the 21st Century has been *The Loose Marbles*.

Why? Because this band has done the most to regenerate our music and to encourage and stimulate the terrific resurgence of traditional jazz among the younger generation (particularly those now based in New Orleans) and because, with the help of YouTube and CDs, it has also encouraged a resurgence of our music throughout the world.

I used to think *The Loose Marbles* were formed in New Orleans after Hurricane Katrina. The truth is, however, that *The Loose Marbles* gave their first performance much earlier - in Providence, Rhode Island, way back in September 2000.

The band was given its name by its founder, the clarinet-player Michael Magro, who grew up in Philadelphia, and he is still running the band today. I have met Michael only once - in New Orleans in April 2016. I found him most friendly, serious-minded and eager to talk about his music.

After all these years, none of his enthusiasm has diminished. Deeply influenced by the recordings of George Lewis, Albert Burbank and Jim Robinson, he is as passionate as ever about the music; and he is clear about how he wants to play it. He puts the emphasis on ensemble work. He prefers the kind of traditional jazz that was played *before* Louis Armstrong and his Hot Five set the fashion for sequences of 'solo' choruses.

Yet Michael did not begin to teach himself the clarinet until he was in his mid-twenties.

Michael told me about those early days. He chose the memorable name *Loose Marbles* partly because of the connotations of the expression but also because the concept of 'looseness' was always part of his plan. This was to be a band without a regular fixed line-up. All good and like-minded musicians would be welcome in his pool of players.

The Band played for a year or so before a break in its history.

Then Michael met Ben Polcer (trumpet and piano). Ben, the son of Ed Polcer, the traditional jazz trumpeter, had graduated at the Music School of the University of Michigan. He joined Michael in the *Loose Marbles* enterprise and has been driving *The Loose Marbles* along ever since. For a while they were based in Brooklyn, New York. In 2006 they developed for a few months by playing street music in Washington Square Park, New York City.

Then, the year after Hurricane Katrina, Michael and Ben permanently relocated to New Orleans, trying their luck by playing for tips on the streets. They have been based there ever since. On occasions, they would return to New York City in the summer months, again giving street performances.

I heard that they sometimes had so many musicians available that there would be two *Loose Marbles* bands in two different locations simultaneously.

During the following three or four years, so many of today's great traditional jazz musicians migrated to New Orleans and appeared as *Marbles*, honing their skills in the company of Ben and Michael. These included such people as Charlie Halloran, Aaron Gunn, Tomas Majcherski, Jason Jurzak, John Rodli, Robert Snow, Jon Gross, Dan Levinson, Alynda Lee Segarra, Kiowa Wells, Ryan Baer, John Royen, Peter Loggins, Robin Rapuzzi, Joseph Faison, Matt Bell, Max Bien-Kahn, Jonathan Doyle and many others. Shaye Cohn frequently worked with the band, but mainly on piano in the early post-Katrina days; and Barnabus Jones, who had recently taken up the trombone (in addition to being already a good violinist and banjo-player), was frequently present. They had a powerful vocalist in Meschiya Lake.

There is a video of considerable historical interest of *The Loose Marbles* in a 2008 configuration, performing at Preservation Hall. You can watch it here:

https://www.youtube.com/watch?v=7Knb2Bz6poE

And see them in the street the same year (with Kiowa singing and Shaye on piano) by going to this YouTube video:

https://www.youtube.com/watch?v=Y1Rjis7Qsow

As dancers also migrated to New Orleans, they tended to join the *Loose Marbles* family too - stars such as Chance Bushman and Amy Johnson; and they became part of the spectacle. The band busked in Europe in 2007: enjoy the dancing by looking at this:

https://www.youtube.com/watch?v=aFmddzu8cto

John and Marla Dixon (later at the heart of *The Shotgun Jazz Band*) arrived a little later, but they too intermingled with the *Marbles* and still work closely with them to this day.

Some of the musicians who played in *The Loose Marbles* have gone on to form bands of their own. Think of *Tom Saunders and the Tom Cats*, for example. And Meschiya Lake, branching out into a wide range of musical styles, now sings with her own very popular band *Meschiya Lake and The Little Big Horns*. Above all, there is *Tuba Skinny*. Shaye Cohn of *Tuba Skinny* has said: 'One thing really important to *The Loose Marbles* was ensemble playing. When I first started with them, I was playing second trumpet. So I had to work to find a voice where I could fit in. It taught me to play very simply, and to listen.'

So *The Loose Marbles* still exists and is attracting plenty of gigs. As the sixty or so musicians who have played in *Loose*

Marbles all still feel part of the family, it is easy enough for Ben and Michael to put together half a dozen of them to play at a gig.

For a really exhilarating video of the band in 2015, try this video. Michael is still in a central rôle, leading off with the melody in the first chorus. Marla is on trumpet and vocal:

https://www.youtube.com/watch?v=BBHn3dtqjos

Interesting to think that, although we fans in our seventies and eighties regard all those musicians currently working so well in New Orleans as the 'young generation', the years seem to have passed so rapidly since Hurricane Katrina that it won't be long before Ben and Michael are considered the 'elder statesmen' of traditional jazz!

THE SHOTGUN JAZZ BAND

Ever since I was overwhelmed by the YouTube video of them playing at The Abita Springs Opry, *The Shotgun Jazz Band* has been one of my favourite groups of musicians. They play a thrilling, raw, no-frills type of traditional jazz. Under the influence of their dynamic leader - Marla Dixon - they are a direct descendant from the bands of Kid Thomas, De De Pierce, Kid Sheik and Kid Howard. Marla learned her jazz by listening to the records of those great trumpet players.

Marla comes from Toronto, where she was also heavily influenced by 'Kid' Cliff Bastien (she met him shortly before he died) and by Patrick Tevlin (who kept *The Happy Pals* band going after Bastien's death and was instrumental in including a lot of younger talented players and introducing them to traditional jazz).

During my visit to New Orleans in April 2015, I managed to attend three concerts by *The Shotgun Jazz Band* and I enjoyed the great privilege of spending some time chatting with them, especially Marla and John Dixon. They were so friendly, generous, kind and willing to talk about their music.

Marla started her working life as a graphic designer. Her husband John (originally from Florida) lived and worked with Marla in Toronto in 2008 before they decided to re-locate to New Orleans.

John had started his musical life by having piano lessons at the age of ten. But in his teenage years he took up the alto saxophone and joined various reading bands - both symphonic and jazz. The music of Duke Ellington was the kind of thing they played. John went on to learning Charlie Parker transcriptions.

But his progress was brought to an abrupt end (the kind all musicians dread) by a serious accident and massive dental damage.

It was not until many years later that he was able to try playing the sax again - but he modestly says he's nowhere near good enough to play it in a traditional jazz band.

So at the time of going to college, he abandoned the saxophone and switched to guitar (mainly electric) and he was soon playing bass guitar in a rock band. After college he formed a country band. John told me he didn't touch a banjo until he met Marla, who bought him his first one while he was staying with her in Toronto. He played it on a gig at Grossman's Tavern with Marla's dixieland band - *The Don Valley Stompers* - and has been hooked ever since. John specialises in a distinctive rock-steady pulsating rhythm, striking all four beats evenly. It's my favourite type of New Orleans rhythm-section playing and it owes much to George Guesnon (1907 - 1968) whose recordings were an inspiration to John.

Marla's technique is perfect for the kind of jazz *The Shotgun Jazz Band* plays. Not only does she find just the right notes (often using sixths, ninths and flattened thirds to add to the excitement); she is a model in timing, phrasing, attack and sheer driving energy. She is also an expert in getting thrilling effects from a mute - especially her aluminium derby mute. I asked whether she inherited that mute from Kid Bastien; but in fact she did not. The Dixons think Bastien's similar mute is now being used by Patrick Tevlin back in Toronto.

As if that isn't enough, Marla knows by heart the words of dozens of songs, without any need to refer to sheets of paper. And she sings with a raw passion and heart-on-sleeve intensity that exactly matches her trumpet playing. *And* she can play the sousaphone - as she often did in the past.

81

It is interesting to trace the evolution of the great *Shotgun Jazz Band*. The seeds were not sown until after John and Marla decided to leave Toronto and try their luck in New Orleans. There, they played as a duet for tips in the streets (mainly at The French Market). They were occasionally joined by a like-minded musician or two. The Dixons happened to arrive in New Orleans at just the right time. There was an amazing resurgence of interest in traditional jazz, with many fine young musicians migrating to that City. John thinks it was significant that dancers arrived too - especially such brilliant dancers as Amy Johnson and Chance Bushman. John told me: 'What followed were more dancers, and with more dancers, more musicians. It was coincidental that Marla and I happened to move here at the same time as this resurgence of interest in traditional jazz. We really had no idea what was going on until we were in it.'

Incidentally, the great reed player Aurora Nealand also told me about the importance for jazz musicians in New Orleans of playing for *dancing*. She thought this did much to explain the special free and relaxed quality of the New Orleans brand of traditional jazz.

By 2011, Marla and John Dixon decided to make a CD, so they hired more players for this purpose and called the resulting band *The Shotgun Jazz Band* because they were living in a shotgun house. What a great choice of name that was. It's immediately striking and memorable. Suddenly they were a proper band, attracting gigs. That first CD (called *Algiers Strut*), with Ben Polcer on piano, happened to include *Love Songs of the Nile*, *I Can't Escape* and *Oriental Man* - all of which are still among the most popular numbers in their repertoire. The second CD (*One Drink Minimum*) did not appear until March 2013 and was recorded during several performances at *The Spotted Cat*. By then, the Dixons had a regular booking there. The CD involved twelve different musicians.

Marla and John's band had no settled personnel at the time. Among the musicians who occasionally played were Christopher Johnson, Michael Magro, Peter Loggins, Orange Kellin, Todd Yannacone, Robert Snow, Benji Bohannon, Tommy Sancton, Aurora Nealand, Jon Gross, Robin Rapuzzi, Barnabus Jones, Craig Flory and several others.

Two more CDs appeared in 2013. And a fifth came out in September 2014. This was *Yearning*, well recorded at Luthjens Dance Hall and demonstrating the high quality of playing they had by then achieved. I think it is the CD of which they are the most proud.

But by then the Band had a reasonably settled line-up and had honed its distinctive sound into the form so many enthusiasts love today.

John pointed out that at Shotgun gigs Marla runs a fairly 'tight ship' and he is proud that their repertoire has become so varied. Of course they play the standards, but, as John says, they also do a lot of 'pop and R&B tunes as well as a few arranged tunes'.

The young Tyler Thomson - one of the world's most exciting players - followed the Dixons to New Orleans from Toronto and joined them on string bass. Tyler's hero was Alcide Pavageau (1888 - 1969); and it shows. It's no surprise that he forms such a great rhythmic engine-room partnership with John Dixon. Justin Peake from Alabama was recruited on drums. His light-touch 4/4 style of playing perfectly complements the strong rhythmic base of the music that Tyler and John provide. Even though Justin went off to college, the Dixons still asked him to play with them whenever he was in town.

The versatile and ubiquitous trombone-player Charlie Halloran from St. Louis played with them a great deal - and still occasionally does. And Haruka Kikuchi - the super young trombonist - moved to New Orleans from Japan at the end of 2013 and settled perfectly into the band - as if it fulfilled her dreams. (She went on to other projects, including running a band of her own.) That superb musician Ben Polcer (originally from New York), long-time friend of the Dixons and an original member of *The Loose Marbles*, is very busy on the New Orleans scene; but he still helps out from time to time with *The Shotgun Jazz Band*, either on piano or - if Marla is unavailable - on trumpet.

Welshman James Evans (reeds) also joined the band at about the same time as Haruka. James told me that when he used to play in the U.K. he would often arrive home from gigs by train in the middle of the night; and that most of his fee would be eaten up by the train fare. He decided to try his luck in New Orleans and his family quickly settled, with his twin children now in school there. He seems to have been snapped up by Marla and John! 'Now,' he said, 'to go to work I have only to walk eight blocks.' As one of the best reed players in the jazz world, James is much in demand and also plays in other New Orleans bands. I could tell that he was a very happy man and really enjoying the fun in working with Marla and John. Just look at him at 3 minutes 26 seconds in this video:

https://www.youtube.com/watch?v=h77s41Q0w5o

With such a virtuoso as James on clarinet and sax, and Haruka Kikuchi or Charlie Halloran on trombone, and Tyler Thomson well established on string bass, the Dixons arrived at a line-up that plays gutsy traditional jazz of the most exciting kind.

They have rapidly risen to be very special and one of the most entertaining traditional jazz bands in the world.

While in town, I spent an evening at *The Maison*, because *The Shotgun Jazz Band* was playing there. Someone in the audience asked Marla to play *Lady Be Good*. I hoped Marla would refuse. I had always thought that tune repetitive and not offering a band much to work on. However, Marla obliged and *The Shotgun Jazz Band* launched into *Lady Be Good*. To my amazement, the excitement built up chorus by chorus until it became one of the most sensational performances of a tune that I heard during my entire stay in New Orleans. (It taught me a lesson: I shall no longer have preconceived dislikes of tunes!) After the applause ended, an English band-leader of my acquaintance, who was sitting at a nearby table, came over to me and said, 'If I died right now, I would die a very happy man!' I know exactly what he meant.

FROM CALYPSOS TO TRADITIONAL JAZZ

Hold Your Hand Madam Khan, *Buy Me a Zeppelin*, *History of Man*, *Seven Skeletons Found in the Yard*, *Roses of Caracas*, *Juliana* - how is it that such tunes have entered the repertoire of the young street bands in New Orleans? It seems that someone on the scene has been deeply affected since early 2014 by Trinidadian calypsos from the 1930s.

Traditional jazz bands have long enjoyed playing an occasional tune with a Latin rhythm. In the standard repertoire, there are *Creole Song* and *Eh La Bas*, *Rum and Coca Cola* and *Mama Inez*, for example; and the minor key section of *St. Louis Blues* and a few tunes such as *Isle of Capri* lend themselves to a Latin beat.

But we have recently seen on YouTube that the bands have revived long-forgotten 1930s calypso numbers. There was the Superband (with Madeleine Reidy on vocal) playing *Hold Your Hand Madam Khan*:

https://www.youtube.com/watch?v=sDVYR39Ptt0

Great fun.

Madeleine kindly sent me this message about a wonderful website from which anyone can obtain inspiration and material: *Here's a music blog I found recently with tons of awesome old calypso (and many other Caribbean genres) recordings uploaded for free:*

http://auraljoy.blogspot.com

The site is indeed tremendous and I pass on Maddie's recommendation to you. My theory is that Madeleine herself is the principal force behind this percolation of Caribbean music into the repertoires of today's bands in New Orleans.

One of the groups in which she plays is *Maddie and Her Calypso Friends*. They recorded *Seven Skeletons Found in the Yard* - a 1938 calypso by Lord Executor (Philip Garcia).

Watch this video:

https://www.youtube.com/watch?v=qyl0w-I9Cak

You can see Madeleine clearly making a speciality of this kind of music.

Watch her singing *Buy Me a Zeppelin* - another great number:

https://www.youtube.com/watch?v=QdXFyyhdHBQ

She has memorised the words of plenty of verses for these songs - no mean feat.

Since 2014 Maddie has led an exciting 12-piece band called *Steamboat Calypso*. Like the great calypso performers of the 1930s (Lord Invader and Roaring Lion, for example), Maddie has given her musicians wonderful stage names - such as Lord Patches, The Duke of Hammers, Porkchop and (Shaye Cohn, no less) The Duchess of Sound. You can find a few videos of the band on YouTube.

The Lionel Belasco tunes *Juliana* and *Roses of Caracas* have been heard on the streets of New Orleans, played by Tuba Skinny. And The Rhythm Wizards included *History of Man* as one of the twelve tracks on their March 2015 CD. More recently we had Tuba Skinny (at the time sharing three players with The Rhythm Wizards) also playing *History of Man* in the street.

The history of the calypso over the last 250 years is very complex. Many influences went into its creation, and in its turn it has spawned music in various sub-genres. If you want to study the history of calypsos in depth, there is plenty to get you started in

Wikipedia. But if you are happy with a few over-simple essentials I can offer you some observations.

The origins of Afro-Caribbean calypsos can be found in the music sung by the slaves of French planters in the Eighteenth Century, especially in Trinidad. The early music had characteristic rhythms and harmonies. The language of the lyrics moved over the years from a form of French creole to a greater intermingling of English. The words were frequently subversive - expressing political satire.

In 1912, on a visit to New York, Lovey's String Band (twelve musicians, including piano, bass, flute, violins, etc. - quite an 'orchestra') made the first recording of a calypso - <u>five years before the first jazz recording</u>! The Lovey String Band and the pianist-composer Lionel Belasco were important names in the recording of the music over the next few years. To my ear, those early recordings seem to use one or two simple repetitive smooth melodic themes, played (for example on violin or clarinet) against a busy rhythmic - almost ragtime – background. There is plenty to sample on YouTube.

Calypsos flourished in the 1920s and 1930s, when the genre became firmly established. Their subject-matter was wide-ranging, but continued to contain much critical comment on politics and society, sometimes under the guise of *double entendre*. Entrepreneurial talent scouts fitted some of the best performers up with impressive stage names and sent them from the West Indies to record and find fame in New York. Principal among them were Roaring Lion (Rafael de Leon), Attila the Hun (Raymond Quevedo), Lord Invader (Rupert Westmore Grant - who composed *Rum and Coca-Cola*), Lord Kitchener (Aldwyn Roberts), Lord Caresser (Rufus Callender) and Wilmoth 'King' Houdini

(Frederick Wilmoth Hendricks).Words were often witty and delivered in rapid-fire style (sometimes extemporised). Listen to Raymond Quevedo and his band performing *Coffee Coffee*. It is hard to imagine *anybody* not enjoying this! In structure, this calypso has much in common with the New Orleans 'Creole' standards *Eh La Bas* and *L'Autre Can Can* (a.k.a. *Creole Song*). But this is unsurprising: they are derived from similar African roots.

From the 1950s, 'toned-down', commercialised calypsos were very much in vogue. There was *The Banana Boat Song*, made famous by Harry Belafonte. And there were films exploiting the craze - notably *Island in the Sun*. The use of steel drums became commonplace. (Ironically, the steel drums have generally been manufactured in European countries, such as Sweden and Switzerland.)

As the repertoire of the Trinidadian band *Codallo's Top Hatters Orchestra* has been revived in New Orleans, it is worth mentioning that band in particular. In the 1930s they recorded *History of Man* and *Hold Your Hand Madam Khan*. And it was Lord Caresser (Rufus Callender) who wrote *Exploiter* (a.k.a. *Buy Me a Zeppelin*).

TUBA SKINNY – WHAT'S THE SECRET?

How do *Tuba Skinny* do it? How is it that this group of surprisingly young musicians – who met in 2009 while busking on the streets of New Orleans, has become the greatest traditional jazz band in the world? Let me offer you twenty-two reasons.

1. They work very hard behind the scenes – researching and learning old material and devising ways of playing it with fresh vigour. And they are perfectionists. Look, for example, at their performances of *Deep Henderson*, a tricky multi-part rhythmic piece. While showing respect for the 1926 recording of this tune by King Oliver's Band, Tuba Skinny do not slavishly imitate: they show what they can do with their own resources. They have arranged the piece meticulously. And all members of the band have the arrangement firmly inside their heads. They know exactly who does what, and when. And they also know where they have a chance to cut loose for a few bars. Now watch other bands playing this tune. Almost invariably they are dependent on printed arrangements of the music on stands in front of them, and their performances sound far less exciting and more stilted.

2. Although Tuba Skinny could play the familiar worn-out tunes of every trad band's repertoire, their programmes mostly comprise exciting unfamiliar gems they have unearthed from the 1920s and 1930s (e.g. *New Orleans Bump, You Can Have My Husband, Chocolate Avenue, Jackson Stomp, Deep Henderson, Banjoreno, Treasures Untold, Russian Rag, Oriental Strut, Minor Drag, Michigander Blues, Harlem's Araby, Me and My Chauffeur, A Jazz Battle, Droppin' Shucks, Fourth Street Mess Around, Carpet Alley Breakdown*). The almost-forgotten artists whose music they have revived include Lucille Bogan, Victoria

90

Spivey, Memphis Minnie, Jabbo Smith, Georgia White, Skip James, Merline Johnson, Ma Rainey, Hattie Hart, The Memphis Jug Band, Blind Blake, Clara Smith, The Dixieland Jug Blowers, The Grinnell Giggers and The Mississippi Mud Steppers; and of course they also play tunes associated with the better-known, such as Bessie Smith, Fats Waller, Louis Armstrong and Jelly Roll Morton. They will surprise you by going to some unconventional sources for tunes they turn into exciting traditional jazz - sources such as Ray Charles and the 21st-century Australian original C. W. Stoneking.

3. All the musicians in the group have thoroughly mastered their instruments; and most of them can play more than one (e.g. cornet + piano + violin; tuba + banjo; trombone + banjo; banjo + harmonica + mandolin + guitar). This provides variety of sound and also the ability to 'substitute' if a regular player is unavailable.

4. They prefer collective improvisation to prima donna solos. Their teamwork is exceptional.

5. They have an outstandingly good singer (Erika Lewis). She has a soulful plaintive voice and great intonation. Her phrasing is perfect and she uses rubato very skilfully. Rather than stick to the familiar jazz standards, she has developed a rich repertoire of tunes rescued from obscurity (e.g. *Tricks Ain't Walking*, *Crow Jane*, *How Do They Do It That Way?*, *Mississippi River Blues*, *I'll See You in the Spring*, *Need a Little Sugar in my Bowl*, *You Let Me Down*, *Got a Man in the 'Bama Mines*, *What's the Matter with the Mill?*). Erika also doubles on bass drum.

6. Other members of Tuba Skinny are also very competent vocalists.

7. The Band rarely uses a conventional percussionist, with full drum kit. Instead, they have a washboard (and sometimes bass

drum). As a result, there is a clean sound to the rhythm. In many traditional jazz bands, the drumming has a smudging effect, filling every space and sometimes forcing other players to blow too loud. Listen to *Tuba Skinny* and you can hear clearly the part played by every single instrument: there is no need to over-blow; and there is none of the muddying effect you sometimes notice with other bands. The washboard player is superb is his energy and inventiveness and time-keeping (and I speak as one who used not to care much for washboards as musical instruments).

8. *Tuba Skinny* avoids the dreary succession of 32-bar 'solo' choruses from four or more instruments that we so often hear in traditional jazz performances. Usually, two or three players lead for a few bars each in covering a 32-bar theme. In the rare instances of complete solo choruses, *Tuba Skinny* musicians add colouring behind the soloist, either with musical phrases or by using stop chords or long notes.

9. *Tuba Skinny* always starts a tune well. The players have devised an appropriate introduction for every one of their tunes.

10. The tuba player Todd Burdick provides a very solid base line for all tunes. It pays from time to time to focus on his contribution and admire its accuracy and solidity.

11. The trombonist Barnabus Jones has absorbed the skills and techniques of the great traditional jazz trombonists in the famous recordings of the 1920s. He and the cornet-player Shaye Cohn work particularly well together – listening carefully to each other and responding to each other's musical phrases. Later-introduced reed players (one of them was English, I'm pleased to say) proved just as skilful.

12. The band takes great care with the setting of tempos at the start of each tune. Once established, the tempo is maintained with

metronomic accuracy. There is none of the speeding up or (worse) the wearying drag-back of tempo that you notice in some bands. The combination of Todd Burdick on tuba and a guitar player (such as Max Bien-Kahn) provides a powerful 'engine' that drives the band along; and all the banjo and guitar players over the years have been brilliant at providing the rock-steady rhythms that our bands require. The banjoists are good at playing tremolos to add emphasis on stressed notes (as in *Jazz Battle*) or to add pretty decorations (to such tunes as *Memphis Shake* and *Michigander Blues*).

13. The Band is not afraid of key changes within tunes, sometimes because the tune is written that way, sometimes to play the tune in a key that suits the whole band and then in a key with which the singer is more comfortable (e.g. *How Do They Do It That Way?* and *Delta Bound* and *Dangerous Blues*) and sometimes just for the mischief of it. Have a listen to *Cannonball*. Notice what tricks they can play even with a 12-bar blues. Admire the Introduction, the Bridges and the Coda, and especially the three key changes! Watch it here:
https://www.youtube.com/watch?v=bkfE_LmHZgU

14. The band devises interesting endings for its tunes. Listen to their very neat codas.

15. The cornet player and (it seems) unofficial director of music, the amazing Shaye Cohn (who is also terrific on piano, violin and accordion - and she even plays the double bass in the country music group *The Lonesome Doves*), is never flashy in her playing. She has a Mozartian instinct for what works best: she contributes to ensembles in the same way that the viola contributes to the 'conversation' in Mozart's string quartets. She can 'bend' notes and knows instinctively when to use this trick to the best

effect. Full of bluesy notes and demonstrating a very effective use of mutes (notably the plunger and the stone-lined cup), the fluent phrases and harmonies she produces are hugely more interesting and exciting than the raucous high-note solos that many traditional jazz trumpeters think the music requires.

16. The Band does not stick doggedly to instrumentation that involves a trumpet (or cornet) - clarinet - trombone front line for every tune. Sometimes, their music has elements of bluegrass or klezmer and this can involve a whole tune (e.g. *Russian Rag*, *Jackson Stomp*, *Papa's Got Your Bath Water On*) being played without cornet or trombone.

17. They don't mind including an occasional waltz in their programme – especially if the tune is beautiful (e.g. *Treasures Untold*, *Sunset Waltz*). These are played lovingly, allowing the melodies to speak for themselves.

18. The violin is sometimes used – both for melodic and rhythmic effects.

19. Members of the Band have composed tunes for their group (e.g. *Salamanca Blues*, *Owl Call Blues* - a hauntingly beautiful song, *Broken-Hearted Blues*, *Thoughts*, the authentically-1920s-sounding *Nigel's Dream*, *Pyramid Strut* - a potential classic of Mortonesque structure and complexity, *Six Feet Down*, the lovely *Blue Chime Stomp* and the craftily-composed *Tangled Blues* - with a highly unusual 18-bar theme). These pieces are fully up to the quality of the material from the 1920s that they love so much.

20. The Band is very skilful with 'breaks' – the element Jelly Roll Morton considered so important in jazz. If you don't know what I mean, I am referring to those phrases (typically two bars) where the whole band stops suddenly, except for one instrument – the clarinet, for example – leaving that player to invent a

decorative musical phrase to fill the gap before the band picks up again. *Tuba Skinny* is particularly good at breaks: there never seems to be any doubt about which player will play the break, and all the players cut off together. (So many other bands fail in this matter. It is particularly irritating when – for example – a drummer plays right through a clarinettist's break.)

21. Tunes do not outstay their welcome: most are completed in about four minutes.

22. Just like a classical orchestra, they take trouble tuning up.

'I think what's unique about our group is that everyone is really dedicated to the music,' said Erika Lewis in an interview. 'That's the bottom line. How we measure success is all about how well we played.'

To sample the band as at late 2016 – in a video with fine sound and visual qualities (we must be grateful to the video-maker codenamed CANDCJ), try this:

https://www.youtube.com/watch?v=NfH2g_yRrpQ

I did not get to hear *Tuba Skinny* in person until The French Quarter Festival in 2015. I had the chance to chat with some of them.

Todd Burdick told me how, after Hurricane Katrina, many young musicians migrated to New Orleans. He moved there from Chicago and he told me that at the time you could find a pal and jointly rent a shotgun house near the French Quarter for just 400 dollars a month. (The price by 2015 had risen to 900 dollars a month.) It was a hard life and some soon gave up. But many settled. They made just enough money to survive by playing for tips on the streets. They started to find like-minded musicians who became their friends and formed themselves into bands. *Loose Marbles* - the band founded by Michael Magro - encouraged promising newcomers to pass through the band's ranks and hone their skills. Many of the musicians who developed their talents in *Loose Marbles* went on to form bands of their own. *Tuba Skinny* is one of those bands.

I had often wondered how *Tuba Skinny* go about unearthing the obscure tunes from the 1920s and 1930s that now form a substantial part of their repertoire. Todd pointed out that it's no longer necessary for someone to have a vintage 78rpm recording. Today there is so much available, not only on re-issued CDs but even on the internet - especially YouTube. For example, the band introduced *Dear Almanzoer* into its repertoire in 2014. This is a lively composition by Oscar 'Papa' Celestin and was recorded in 1927 by his band. Thanks to the kindness of various YouTube uploaders, Todd said, you can freely listen to - and learn from - the Celestin original.

I asked whether the members of *Tuba Skinny* get together for private rehearsals occasionally. After all, some of their music is tricky, with complicated arrangements. Think of *Cannonball Blues* as a typical example: with so many surprising key changes and various ensemble phrasing patterns to remember, you can't just turn up and play such a tune. Everybody needs to have learned exactly what their rôle is at any given point. Robin told me much of the experimenting and 'rehearsing' takes place on the street. They like to play in Royal Street twice a week if possible. But they *do* also have an occasional rehearsal in one of their houses, perhaps once a month. They had recently been rehearsing once a week - but this was in the lead-up to the recording of their seventh CD - *Blue*

Chime Stomp. The recording took place over two days in early April 2015.

I asked about the 'arranging' of the more complex of *Tuba Skinny*'s tunes. It seems obvious that Shaye Cohn is the expert in this matter and has a big say (though she modestly claimed she does not need to do much other than 'direct the traffic' in performance). I was assured that the band's decisions are 'democratic' and that all contribute ideas, though it's a fact that Shaye will sometimes supply a 'chart', especially for banjo and guitar players.

I mentioned *Maple Leaf Rag* as an example. It had been recently introduced into *Tuba Skinny*'s repertoire and obviously they had to decide in which key to play it (some bands go for Eb moving into Ab; but Tuba Skinny chose F going into Bb). They also had to make up their minds about which of the tune's four possible melodic themes they should play and in which order, and whether with any distinctive treatments. And they had to decide whether to include an introduction, bridges and a coda. If you watch this video, you will see what they came up with:

https://www.youtube.com/watch?v=kYJhgz4L3UU

Enjoy especially the use of those long harmonising notes in the final choruses preceding the out-chorus. When they played *Maple Leaf Rag* at The French Quarter Festival a few weeks later, with slightly different personnel, the arrangement was essentially the same, though with two fewer of the 16-bar final choruses, and also this time there was a two-bar coda - I guess a spur-of-the-moment Shaye-ism that took nobody by surprise!

Todd told me he had recently deputised in another band which had also played *Maple Leaf Rag*. But their version turned out to be quite different from *Tuba Skinny*'s. Did this cause him any difficulty? No. He said he easily picked up what was going on.

I saw Tuba Skinny playing in a very crowded bar. I assumed the great number of people had all gone there specially to hear the band. I was wrong. I was trapped in the middle of the crowd near the bar, unable to move and quite a few yards from the stage. But when the band started to play, I found the din of conversation around me was so loud that I could hardly hear the music. And so it continued. I felt so disappointed for the musicians, even more than for myself: they were producing such wonderful music and yet only a few people near the stage could hear them clearly. When I eventually met Shaye, I told her how sorry I was that the band had been treated in this way. She shrugged her shoulders philosophically and said, 'Well, it's a bar....'.

But no wonder the band still so much enjoys playing in the street, where they can be clearly heard and be given respect by people who love their music.

I had constantly wondered how Shaye manages to create all those wonderful phrases she plays (often with a mute) as a backing to Erika's vocals and also in support when the trombone or clarinet takes the melody. I asked her whether, while playing, she was thinking her way through the chords. She paused to consider my question for a moment, as if she had never thought about the process before. Yes, she knew the chords all right; but she felt that her inventions had become 'intuitive'.

In chatting with Barnabus, I got on to the unlikely topic of diminished chords. When I hummed a particularly enjoyable phrase he had played over a diminished chord in a YouTube video some years ago, he remembered exactly the one I meant and said he had picked the phrase up from Ewan Bleach!

98

One evening I bumped into that brilliant and ubiquitous trombonist Charlie Halloran. When he told me he would be playing with *Tuba Skinny* the following night (deputising during a rare absence of Barnabus Jones), I asked him how he would cope with *Tuba Skinny*'s often complex arrangements. What if they played *Deep Henderson*, for example? He said *Deep Henderson* would be no trouble, as he knew their arrangement well. However, he told me 'I expect they will dumb down the programme a bit to make allowances for me.' Well, I went to the concert. And I can tell you this: *Tuba Skinny* did not 'dumb down' at all. They played a typical programme, complex arrangements included. And how did Charlie cope? Brilliantly. He played some wonderful stuff and, as far as I could tell, never put a foot wrong.

I enjoyed observing how Shaye prepares a playlist. At The French Quarter Festival, for a quarter hour before the performance started, she sat in her place looking at her notebooks and working out a programme. She wrote the tune titles with a chunky marker pen on a sheet of paper which she then placed on the floor in the centre of the band, so that all members could know what was coming next. I noticed how skilfully she made the programme entertaining by alternating slower and quicker tunes, and mixing instrumental with vocal numbers, and even ensuring a variety of keys.

Watching *Tuba Skinny* perform their specials - such as *Freight Train Blues* and the new ones by Shaye - *Tangled Blues* and *Blue Chime Stomp* - it was such a joy to observe at close quarters how brilliant they all are, and such perfectionists.

At the time of writing, *Tuba Skinny* have recorded 7 CDs. Although they have appeared elsewhere in the USA, notably in New York, and also toured in several countries, including Mexico,

Sweden, Australia, Switzerland, France, Italy and Spain, they spend half their year busking in the streets and playing in the clubs of New Orleans, their natural setting.

In the French Quarter, they use bicycles for all transport needs.

How do they decide on their repertoire? In an interview, washboard-player Robin Rapuzzi explained: *It's a group decision. It always is. Tuba Skinny is a miniature political system of majority rule. We discuss ideas with each other either on the street or over dinner. We have listening-parties throughout the year to discuss what we're interested in and where we want to go with our music. It's very organic. We're very fortunate to all be so interested in the same kind of music and to have met each other when and where we did and with a travelling itch and desire to busk.*

In the streets, there is no use of the electronic amplification that spoils so much music these days.

For its first three years, the band had no reed player (except when a welcome guest sat in), so there was a distinctive brassy sound.

Erika Lewis, originally from New York State's Hudson Valley not only has an amazingly strong and soulful voice, ideal for the blues; her control of pitch and command of rubato are perfect. She has been compared with Bessie Smith (who must have been her inspiration) and in my opinion she equals the great Bessie in vocal ability. In street performances she needs no microphone. From 2012, Erika took to playing the bass drum, on which she sits as she sings and plays - further solidifying the band's rhythm section. Erika has said (Offbeat Magazine, September 2014), 'It just dawned on me one day that a bass drum was something that I could add and it would fit in. For the first year, I strapped it to my front, but I felt like a pregnant spider flailing around, standing up while everyone else was sitting down. So I said, *I'm just going to sit down on it.*'

There is a vocal in about 75% of the tunes played by the band, and these are mostly sung by Erika.

At the end of 2015, to the disappointment of her many fans, Erika moved away from New Orleans and therefore ceased appearing with the band in the New Orleans streets. But she continued to appear with the band at festivals and on tours.

Tuba Skinny is a model collective enterprise, without a star or prima donna. But I must admit a special admiration of Shaye Cohn, the young lady who plays the cornet and generally directs the musical traffic. As one who attempts to play the jazz cornet myself, I appreciate her technical virtuosity and amazing inventiveness. Her phrasing is impeccable. Her playing is busy, but in an unobtrusive way. Just listen to her extraordinarily inventive and subtle improvisations and don't miss the way she provides those brilliant delicate arabesques behind the solos of others (such as the trombone - which often takes the melody), and particularly behind the singer.

I have been told that, when she was just nine years old, Shaye was a member of The New England Conservatory Children's Chorus and sang solo on stage. This amazing lady from Boston is classically trained and, as YouTube demonstrates, also plays other instruments (especially the accordion, violin and piano - and even the spoons!) brilliantly. To judge from videos and recordings, Shaye is currently also one of the best traditional jazz piano-players on the New Orleans scene. She even does the delightful artwork for the band's CDs. She is so talented!

The guitarist when the band was formed was Kiowa Wells and he and the slim Todd Burdick (tuba - Mr. Tuba Skinny in person - originally from Chicago) were the founders of the band, building it up by inviting other fine musicians they met busking on the streets of New Orleans. They originally worked (circa 2007) in the band *Loose Marbles*, the great musical collective that still exists but that spawned several of the great bands based in New Orleans today. Todd and Kiowa are very skilful, sensitive and accurate players. You quickly notice from their first recordings how thoroughly they have learned their music, how meticulously they prepare and play. Todd originally played guitar and banjo (as he still does when required) and he is very good on those instruments. It must be a big help to be strong in your knowledge of chord sequences when laying a secure foundation on the tuba.

Kiowa occasionally sang; and he also contributed some fine guitar solo choruses. Listen carefully to the tuba in those early Tuba Skinny performances (available on YouTube) and notice how solid and accurate is the foundation Todd lays and how important this is to the special sound of the band.

It seems that Ryan Baer on banjo and guitar replaced Kiowa after a year or so. Ryan is extremely good, whether providing rhythmic support or delicate melodic solo choruses. He too is a fine singer.

And in later months, other guitar and banjo players have been frequently used. Guitarist Max Bien-Kahn from Oregon, who has also frequently worked as the band's recording engineer, has provided a rock-solid rhythmic backing in many performances, and toured with the band. In 2014 such fine and well-known New Orleans street performers as Gregory Sherman and Jason Lawrence (and occasionally Stalebread Scottie) played on banjo and guitar. Another fine player who appears frequently on tenor banjo is the Texan Westen Borghesi. To appreciate Westen's very skilful and sympathetic playing, listen carefully to his contribution throughout the band's CD called *Pyramid Strut*.

No matter who plays, they all conform to the *Tuba Skinny* house style - laying down a very solid four-to-the-bar foundation. The combination of Todd Burdick on tuba and a guitar player (such as Max Bien-Kahn) provides a powerful engine that drives the band along; and all the banjo players over the years have been brilliant at providing that rock-steady rhythm that our bands require.

Trombonist Barnabus Jones possesses a big sound and has mastered the tricks of Kid Ory, John Thomas, Honoré Dutrey and Fred Robinson - the trombonists who played with Louis Armstrong in the 1920s. Barnabus produces musical phrases that perfectly complement the melodic inventions of Shaye Cohn. The trombone and cornet blend magically.

What is more, he too (from evidence I have seen) is also brilliant on other instruments - the banjo and the violin, which were his original instruments; and on occasion he shows himself to be no mean singer!

All the *Tuba Skinny* instruments are easily portable. This is particularly helpful if you are a street band. Washboard player Robin Rapuzzi from Seattle (though I'm proud to report his mother was born in England!) is a great driving force for the rhythm of this band, and fully underpins the music's structures. He has fixed a few additional small percussive items to his washboard, so he can produce tricky crowd-pleasing solo choruses, with sound varied very imaginatively. Although it's easier to play a washboard on the street than to lug around a full drum kit, Robin is in fact a drummer, and enjoys the full range of tones and colours that he can get from the drum kit, including the snare and Chinese tom-drum and Chinese-crash cymbal. He used a full drum kit when making the band's 7th CD; and at the end of 2015 he managed to start taking his full kit along to street busking - using a bicycle with a trailer - which he described as 'some kind of work out'!

There are other part-time members of this band – too numerous for me to track or mention. In their videos you may spot an occasional double bass, or violin, or a second trumpet. This is bound to happen with a street busking band. But I must tell you that a young lady called Alynda Lee Segarra (who now mostly works with her own band) used to play banjo and sing (very well). But most of the fine young musicians of New Orleans have played in the band at some time or other.

Ewan Bleach from the U.K. on clarinet and saxophone fitted in brilliantly for a year or so (Ewan is incidentally also a superb jazz pianist); and John Doyle on sax and clarinet is another fine player (reminiscent of Jimmy Noone) who settled well into the band during 2013 when they were playing some of their greatest music. These two are outstandingly good musicians. Just listen closely to their work in any of the videos and you will class them among the very best traditional jazz reedmen you have ever encountered.

Jonathan Doyle studied briefly at Depaul's School of Music in Chicago and has worked with several bands, including his own quintet. He now divides his time between Chicago, Austin and spells with *Tuba Skinny* - in New Orleans and touring abroad. He is also a composer of music for his bands.

By the way, as well as playing in *Tuba Skinny*, Jonathan Doyle and Westen Borghesi both play in the wonderful *Thrift Set*

Orchestra in Austin, Texas. There are some videos of this group - well worth watching - on YouTube.

From 2014 onwards, the reed player has usually been Craig Flory, from Seattle. And by the end of 2015, the very fine player Tomas Majcherski was regularly helping out on reeds.

Tuba Skinny dresses and presents itself in a laid-back, casual manner. The gents wear baseball caps and – on hot days – play in singlets and shorts, without shirts. The ladies have a penchant for short socks and flat shoes or trainers. So they have perfect looks for a New Orleans street band; and they tend to dress in just the same way for indoor gigs – bringing a breath of fresh air into what might otherwise be stuffy or formal venues.

They are modest, unassuming young people, having fun playing the music they love and scarcely aware of their own enormous talent.

One of my American friends urged me to watch a video which, he said, 'shows why they are the best band in the world!' The band while visiting Italy was playing Jelly Roll Morton's *Grandpa's Spells* (1923). Their interpretation (in the key of C, going into F for the Trio) is vigorous and enterprising, working as much round the chords as on the melody and making a great use of breaks: Morton himself would have been very impressed! I guess Shaye must have played a big part in the arrangement. One of the delights of this video is the absorbed expressions on the faces of the children watching the band. You can enjoy the performance superbly filmed by Salar Golestanian by going here and then clicking on the arrow:

https://vimeo.com/101422951

But please let me beg you to explore this band's performances for yourself! There are over 450 examples of their work on YouTube.

By the way, you can help support these wonderful young musicians by obtaining one or more of their CDs. You can buy or download them online. You can pay with PayPal. It works even from other countries, as I have found. Start by going to their website and that tells you how to go about it:

http://tubaskinny.tk/

JENAVIEVE COOKE

If you would like to see a performance by a remarkable young lady who is a singer / trumpet-player / band-leader (and very good in all three rôles), go to:

https://www.youtube.com/watch?v=m2sQ0JIbXdY

Giving up a good career to become a musician, especially when it means learning new instruments from scratch, can be 'hard and scary'. That's what Jenavieve Cooke told me. And having got to know her, I can easily understand what she meant. She said that although it is hard and scary it is also 'very exciting and rewarding'.

The first time I heard of Jenavieve Cooke was in August 2015, when a friend suggested I should watch some YouTube videos in which she was featured. With her Band - *The Royal Street Winding Boys* - she was filmed busking in New Orleans. She played trumpet on *That's a Plenty* and also sang numbers such as *Egyptian Ella*.

I was hooked. Jenavieve had a band of very fine musicians, and she presented the music in a forthright, appealing way. She also had charisma, and what you might call 'stage presence'.

So, when I visited New Orleans in 2016, I sought out Jenavieve's band.

I must pass on what I learned from Jenavieve about her development as a musician. It is a fascinating story that would make a novel in itself; and I think it illustrates so well the *drive, bravery, dedication and hard work* to be admired in the new young generation of traditional jazz musicians who have migrated to New Orleans.

Jenavieve was born in Bremerton in Washington State. (If your geography is as bad as mine, it may help to picture that as pretty well 120 miles south of Vancouver in Canada.) Her father was a naval officer on the base there. It wasn't long before the family found itself on the opposite side of the USA, in Annapolis, Maryland, where there is a big naval base to which her father had been transferred. This was one of many moves that must have disrupted Jenavieve's education. She told me she changed schools eight times during twelve years. Her father would be at sea for months at a time.

Throughout her childhood, Jenavieve knew that she had music in her soul.

Soon, her father having left active duty to be in the Reserves, they moved to Orlando, Florida. When Jenavieve was only 12, her mother became seriously ill with cancer and successfully underwent chemotherapy.

Her parents arranged for her to have piano lessons, but only for six months. Jenavieve also played drums in the band of one of the Middle Schools that she attended briefly.

At High School, Jenavieve underwent a rigorous International Baccalaureate programme. This left her no time to join one of the school bands. But she was always singing: 'I used to sing constantly in my room or in school and my brother always told me to shut up whenever I sang!'

She told me 'My dad wanted me to be a doctor or a lawyer and my mom was very sick. That was the moment I decided I would never be a musician, but rather a music lover.'

However, in the late 1990s, while at High School, Jenavieve got into swing dancing. She also discovered the recordings of Louis Armstrong and Billie Holiday. And such visiting bands as the

Squirrel Nut Zippers (from Asheville) thrilled her and showed what was possible. 'I was in love with it all. It spoke to my soul in a very unpretentious and permanent way.'

Jenavieve went to university, studying medicine for two years before deciding this was not for her and switching to a further two years double-majoring in Advertising and Psychology, while at the same time taking lots of art classes. She moved to San Francisco where, after further study, she found a job in which she could be truly creative: art direction in advertising. She loved the job ...... and yet still didn't feel content with her life.

One weekend a group of young musicians passed through. She was so moved by the joy they experienced and gave. This was the crucial moment. She gave up her job, bought a guitar and headed to Costa Rica with a one-way ticket.

Then she spent *seven years* travelling extensively in Canada, Central America and Europe. She played the guitar, learned music, busked, hitch-hiked, camped, worked on farms, made and sold leather goods, picked up languages, and recorded music from various cultures. She told me 'I travelled pretty much penniless'. Jenavieve believes all of this was a massively beneficial experience.

(You see what I mean about Jenavieve's life sounding like the plot of a substantial novel.)

She was 25 when she started to learn to play the trumpet. (She can now also play various other instruments, including the accordion). The Jenavieve Cooke of today began to emerge.

She worked immensely hard at her trumpet playing and in developing her vocal skills.

Between working in Europe and elsewhere, Jenavieve regularly spent a few months in New Orleans. A speciality of hers was traditional Balkan music. And in fact she has never lost this interest: she has founded in New Orleans a Balkan Brass Band called *Backyard Belladonna*.

In the summer of 2013 she attended the famous Welbourne Traditional Jazz Camp, where the tutors include some of the greatest New Orleans-based musicians.

Then she settled in New Orleans, determined to 'really learn this traditional jazz stuff'! She formed her band *The Royal Street Winding Boys* (and what an appropriate and memorable Jelly Roll Morton-inspired name she chose for it!). Despite the struggles familiar to any band trying to get itself recognised, she now has the satisfaction of seeing her band firmly established in the local scene.

Jenavieve told me: 'I will probably be struggling the rest of my life but somehow it seems worth it. It's about the people we touch, all the people who benefit from the music we're playing. Just how I am touched and was changed by the music I hear.'

Jenavieve's concert with *The Royal Street Winding Boys* that I attended was extremely enjoyable. She played not only standards such as *After You've Gone* and *I've Found a New Baby* but also some of the obscurer numbers from long ago, such as *Fourth Street Mess Around*, *Do Your Duty*, *Bogalusa Strut*, *Delta Bound*, *Mean Blue Spirits* and *Michigander Blues*. Arrangements of the tunes were neat and uncomplicated. Wherever possible, she included the verses as well as the choruses of familiar songs; and she had some interesting head arrangements (for instance, switching in to double-time occasionally for a middle eight). She fronted the band with that excellent stage presence that I had noted in the videos. She had become a very good singer indeed and also a confident trumpet player, able to state a melody with a little tasteful decoration and then in later choruses to improvise lustily and fluently. Jenavieve also led well and gave her fellow musicians plenty of opportunities to display their skills. It is not surprising that some of the best local musicians feel privileged to have been invited to be *Royal Street Winding Boys*.

She is a fine entertainer with a fine band. If you are ever in New Orleans, may I urge you to seek them out?

Although the conditions (dim lighting and background noise) made filming far from ideal, I videoed the band. You may view the result here:

https://www.youtube.com/watch?v=YX2L3Qh3urA

'YES MA'AM' - THE GREAT STRING BAND

During my April 2016 visit to New Orleans, I was thrilled at last to hear the string band *Yes Ma'am*. I had admired their work on YouTube for several years.

I found them playing at The French Market. What a dazzling performance! I can assure you they are even more exciting in person than when seen on YouTube. Each musician individually is a virtuoso. The finger-work on some of the solo choruses was mind-boggling. The songs were witty; and the control of 'breaks' and rhythm (sometimes doubling-up) was so clever and effective. You can't help having a big smile on your face and you can't stop your feet tapping when *Yes Ma'am* are playing.

At the break, I was fortunate enough to have a chat with the leader - Matt Bracken. On YouTube, Matt (like *Yes Ma'am* in general) has always given me the impression of being very laid-back, devil-may-care, unconventional and bohemian in life-style. Well, maybe some of that is true. But I have to report that the man I met that day was also deadly serious about his music, modest, very articulate, extremely hard-working and also kind and generous in talking with me.

I thanked Matt for the pleasure his band had given to YouTube viewers all over the world. I told him I was amazed at his own brilliance and versatility: he sits at the centre of the band, playing the guitar with great vigour and lustily singing, while simultaneously providing percussion: with his feet he plays a 'drum' and a tambourine and a bell! In the course of a performance he uses a huge amount of energy.

He very modestly said he did not consider himself a great player. In his opinion, the rest of the band were the technically-gifted players and he was privileged to have them working with him.

Well, there you have the recipé for a perfect team: a leader who is a dedicated, tireless, directing presence surrounded by other musicians whom he respects and encourages to display their skills.

Those *Yes Ma'am* songs tend to be tricky in structure. Think of the sudden tempo changes. How does the band get to perform them so slickly? And where do the songs come from?

Matt's answers were surprising. He told me he himself now composes about 90% of the material. The band hones and masters it during their many performances on the streets.

I had guessed they must get together from time to time to rehearse. No, Matt told me. He could recall that they had had two rehearsals. No more.

But is all this really traditional jazz? Yes, it certainly is. The links and overlaps between jug bands and string bands and what has become 'conventional' traditional jazz (with a front line of trumpet, trombone and clarinet) go right back to the earliest days; and they have been gloriously revived by the young musicians in the New Orleans today. Instrumentation in the string bands may be slightly different (though I should mention that *Yes Ma'am* sometimes includes a cornet and trombone), but the principles for playing and interpreting the music are exactly the same.

In the years during which Matt's band has been evolving, there have been several changes of personnel (and I believe he still draws from a pool of players). Two of the three original ladies are still in the band. When I saw them in April 2016, I made a video and I invite you to watch it:

https://www.youtube.com/watch?v=Owz7P3l9joI

There are plenty of videos of the band on YouTube. One of my favourites from their earlier days (2011) is this:

https://www.youtube.com/watch?v=tbbVXKiHXns

Whatever you think, please watch right to the end: there are surprises along the way. And admire all the little details.

TYLER THOMSON

Let's play Fantasy Traditional Jazz. Imagine you have to put together your 'dream' band - drawn from the very best musicians alive today. Who would you have on string bass?

I can tell you I would pick the young Canadian Tyler Thomson.

Tyler comes from Toronto where he mastered his trade with *The Happy Pals Band*. His inspiration was the great New Orleans bassist Alcide Pavageau (1888-1969), who recorded with the bands of George Lewis and Bunk Johnson in the 1940s and who also played in the early days of Preservation Hall.

Tyler is sensationally good, whether he is playing a sympathetic background in a slow number, or pounding a solid 4/4 in a pulsating performance of a quick tune. For a fine example of his work, look at this video:

https://www.youtube.com/watch?v=RicINWvmAcg

Note his dazzling solo chorus in *Oriental Man*. It comes at 17 minutes 36 seconds. It's heartening to think he was only 25 years old at the time of this performance.

As you can see, Tyler plays now in *The Shotgun Jazz Band*. When I met him during my visit to New Orleans in April 2015, he told me he had gone to New Orleans 'for a vacation' in 2013 and had stayed ever since.

Of course this was one of his jokes. I quickly discovered three things about Tyler:

(1) Offstage, he hardly ever stops joking. In fact, all members of *The Shotgun Jazz Band* are constantly joking, teasing and laughing and I'm sure this is one reason why they strike anyone who meets them as a 'happy family' as well as a happy band.

115

(2) He is so modest about his music-making that it's impossible to get him to talk seriously about it.

(3) Tyler is obsessed by sport - both as a player and a spectator. Sometimes, between tunes, you see him on his cell-phone catching up on the latest scores. He broke his foot playing basketball early in 2015 and was going around on crutches (but still playing gigs) for quite a while.

So Tyler will tell you he has been playing string bass since his late teenage years but still has no idea what he is doing, apart from having fun.

Having followed Marla and John Dixon to New Orleans, he joined them playing on the streets, where they already had the nucleus of today's *Shotgun Jazz Band*. They made CDs and started to get invitations to play in the clubs, bars and festivals. By 2015, they were so busy with bookings (averaging five a week) that they no longer needed to busk. Tyler is pleased about that. He found the street work increasingly tiring, especially when - because of the competition - it became so hard to secure a good spot.

Despite his jokes, Tyler clearly knows exactly what he is doing when he is playing. He doesn't put a foot wrong or hit an incorrect chord while maintaining a rock-steady four-beats-to-the-bar (sometimes eight) bass line. I have never seen him refer to a chord book. He has internalised the chord sequences of a huge range of tunes.

It's not surprising that this exciting player is now much in demand. He is booked by such long-established greats as Michael White and Greg Stafford to play in their bands from time to time.

So since 2014, Tyler has been playing about five gigs a week, mainly with *The Shotgun Jazz Band*.

And (like so many of the young New Orleans musicians) Tyler can also play a second instrument - in his case the piano. And he is a pretty good singer. You can find evidence of all this on YouTube.

CONRAD, CHLOE, AND JUSTIN

A few years ago, a friend asked me to have a look at the video of Chloe Feoranzo and Conrad Cayman playing and singing the duet *What Are You Doing New Year's Eve?*

I had not previously heard of Chloe and Conrad but I was immediately enchanted. It must be one of the sweetest performances by just two musicians ever to appear on YouTube. If you haven't yet seen the video, please have a look:

https://www.youtube.com/watch?v=O3w8aI5Jd0Q

Isn't that one of the sweetest performances you have ever heard?

But after that touching, gentle performance (in 2012), fast forward to April 2016 and watch Chloe playing the C melody sax, trading bars at high speed with James Evans. The final couple of minutes of this video (the last four choruses) are sensational:

https://www.youtube.com/watch?v=rTFXYDyBRr4

On that evidence (Chloe had just moved to New Orleans a few days earlier and this was her first full gig with the band) I would say Chloe was at that time the best and most exciting traditional jazz reed player aged under 25 in the world. She is brilliant on saxes and clarinet *and* also plays ukulele *and* she sings most beautifully. What a talented young lady!

And then, for more excitement, watch both Conrad and Chloe in the same week playing *Fidgety Feet* in New Orleans with The Shotgun Jazz Band:

https://www.youtube.com/watch?v=oZ_oWWqzq5I

I had the great pleasure of meeting both Conrad and Chloe when I was in New Orleans. Conrad was involved in several musical ventures and had recently gone full-time as a musician and band-leader. Chloe has been playing trad jazz festivals since the age of 15. She went off to college in St. Louis but decided to drop out after only two years because her career had taken over: she had so many attractive gigs in her diary that she was too busy to go on attending lessons! Roots American artist Pokey LaFarge had spotted her playing with a local band and asked her to tour with his band. She did that for three years, travelling all over the world.

In April 2016, she took the decision to move home to New Orleans and was immediately in demand to play with several bands. I guessed she would stay happy and extremely busy. And Chloe does not feel that she is exclusively a traditional jazz player. She also plays modern as well as various ethnic folk styles.

Earlier in California, Conrad and Chloe, together with trumpet-player Justin Au, had been the nucleus of a small group calling itself The JC Jazz Crew. May I suggest you check out their website: www.jcjazzcrew.com. And have a look at this charming video:

https://www.youtube.com/watch?v=7FvSoxSwyi8

Justin comes from a famous jazzing family. He and his brothers Gordon and Brandon have also been playing traditional jazz since their youth. They were influenced by their uncle, Howard Miyata, who plays tuba and trombone with The High Sierra Jazz Band. Justin has played and recorded with many of the 'big names' of today; and he also works in Sacramento, teaching music and traditional jazz on various youth programmes.

These three young people made some great videos in Conrad's living room. Curiously enough, they really enjoyed sitting on the floor to play. So when they recorded a CD, they called it *Four on the Floor* (including Conrad's vacuum cleaner, which happens to feature in some of the videos!). Conrad very kindly gave me a copy of the CD and both he and Chloe autographed it for me. What a souvenir!

The CD is a delight. For example, there's an astonishing number of clever touches to enjoy in *Riverboat Shuffle*, which they take at quite a pace. With a guest on four of the eleven tracks, and vocals on five tracks, there is technically brilliant music in a variety of moods, with some slick arrangements. The very popular Katie Cavera on banjo and bass is one of the guests; the other is Corey Gemme on trombone (though elsewhere he also plays reeds, cornet, sousaphone *and* is a composer!).

Conrad explained to me that, because he and Justin live six hours apart, and Chloe was touring, the three friends got together only once or twice a year, including November for the San Diego Jazz Festival. Just for fun, they made a video, playing the *Stars Wars Cantina Band Song*. Amazingly, at the time of my typing, it has been viewed almost a quarter of a million times.

These modest young people are altogether charming and amazingly talented. Let us look forward to many years of great music from them.

THE BALKAN BRASS BAND INFLUENCE

My American friend and frequent correspondent Phil is very keen on a band called *The California Feetwarmers*. You can hear this band of very proficient musicians at:

https://www.youtube.com/watch?v=RkgEMy57yk8

where they play slick arrangements of *Aunt Hagar's Blues*, *San* and *Bill Bailey*.

Phil told me some of the players previously played as a 'Balkan brass band' and there is still a great influence of the disciplines of Balkan brass band music in their playing.

This set me thinking, because Balkan Brass Band Music is something about which I knew virtually nothing. So I spent a couple of hours reading about it. It seems to have arisen from the folk music mainly of Serbia, Macedonia and Bulgaria. Much of the music supports vigorous dancing. It has repetitive insistent melodies and very strong rhythms.

Picture a village square where colourfully-dressed dancers in a circle, hands linked, dance in a manner that involves fast-paced complicated foot movements while the upper bodies remain statuesque. They are accompanied by a sousaphone heavily stamping the first and third beats of the bars, an accordion playing rapid sequences of notes, a violin, trumpets and other horns, as well as sundry busy percussion instruments. The band plays with technical precision. The harmonies sound simple – largely involving the three main chords (but perhaps this is deceptive, since it seems likely also that they using some uncommon scales); and the melodies, mostly rapid, contain some acrobatic twists and turns. In some tunes, there are compound time signatures, notably 9/8 and 7/8.

121

I learned that there are various song forms of which the two commonest are the Kolo and the Čoček. Both can be in the tricky 9/8 rhythmic form.

To get an immediate feel for what Balkan brass band music at its brassiest sounds like, go to:

https://www.youtube.com/watch?v=10pn4OH2GrA

The Balkan influence has spread among the best traditional jazz musicians of today. Think of Jenavieve Cooke. In her years of nomadic living, she picked up Balkan music at its source.

Years before she formed the famous *Royal Street Winding Boys*, Jenavieve founded in New Orleans a Balkan brass band called *Backyard Belladonna*.

And there's Ben Schenk (mainly playing clarinet), now in his 50s, who spent years evolving the kind of band that seemed just right for him. He ended up with *The Panorama Jazz Band*, which is quite capable of playing traditional jazz in familiar style, but also has in its programmes doses of influence from Balkan brass band music and Klezmer music, not to mention a considerable Caribbean element! Panorama has been a truly great band since Aurora Nealand (who, by the way, has toured in the Balkans) joined it. She - one of the world's greatest reed players - has a heart full of the joys of music of all cultures. She perfectly complements Ben's work. There are plenty of videos of the band on YouTube but I will mention this one, where you catch them in Big Band Mardi Gras format:

https://www.youtube.com/watch?v=uCfNSK-GtQM

And think of Matt Schreiber. This fine accordion player and Balkan music specialist not only plays with Ben in the *Panorama Jazz Band* but also works in the specialist *Mahala Trio* (Balkan music in New Orleans). Try watching a video of him and his two colleagues here:

https://www.youtube.com/watch?v=GSVh9efRkEk

It's not a brass band but it certainly gives novices such as myself a good insight into the nature of Balkan music.

And now we have *The Wit's End Brass Band*. They have produced a remarkable CD that you can find on Bandcamp. You really must watch this video of them:

https://www.youtube.com/watch?v=K-0zyZGpXTw

I discovered there are many 'Balkan Bands' all over the world, even in such unlikely places as England, Australia and the Netherlands. In the USA there are dozens of them, and Balkan Band Summer Camps are held on both the East and West Coasts. For a terrific Balkan SuperBand playing in our beloved Royal Street, New Orleans, try this:

https://www.youtube.com/watch?v=KPc1cmkK-0k

In spirit, instrumentation and rhythmic excitement, it seems to me this Balkan music has a lot in common with Klezmer music, which has also had a permeating influence on New Orleans jazz in the 21st Century. Add to these influences that of Caribbean calypso music – much associated in recent years with *The Panorama Jazz Band* and with Madeleine Reidy and later with *The Rhythm Wizards* in New Orleans and - Wow! We observe some very interesting developments in the music we love.

SHAYE COHN: COMPOSER

Multi-instrumentalist band-leader Shaye Cohn is considered by many to be the best and most important traditional jazz musician anywhere in the world. So you must excuse me if I seem to be referring a great deal to her achievements. Right now I want to consider her contribution as a composer.

Still only in her early 30s, Shaye has already given us the very entertaining and clever *Blue Chime Stomp*. Remember the haunting *Owl Call Blues*. And there was *Salamanca Blues* - a lovely melancholy piece with themes in F and then Ab, giving plenty of opportunities to the trombone and banjo. The medium-tempo *Tangled Blues* is a particularly clever composition: as its title suggests, it sets us plenty to 'untangle', with pretty, wistful phrases popping up in different keys and in two different themes - one of which runs for the highly unusual length of 18 bars. Then there is the mighty Mortonesque *Pyramid Strut*, composed while the band Tuba Skinny was touring in Australia. This is the most complex of Shaye's creations. It has four themes, as well as an 8-bar bridge, and uses two keys. Lots of 'breaks' are built in and there are witty moments - such as the Coda. You can find videos of all these tunes on YouTube.

Shaye's composition *Nigel's Dream* sounds so authentically 1920s that you could easily be fooled into thinking it was a previously undiscovered manuscript by King Oliver.

You can hear Shaye and Tuba Skinny performing *Nigel's Dream* here:

https://www.youtube.com/watch?v=-mH63AsRRuw

As ever, we must be grateful to the video-maker (in this case *RaoulDuke504*) for bringing this tune to our attention.

Its cheeky two-bar introduction involves nothing more than one 'Charleston' bar from the washboard followed by a single chord from the banjo, guitar and tuba. Then we are into Theme A - 32 bars in the key of C. Great use is made of a phrase (reminiscent of the Middle Eight of *East Coast Trot*) in which a flattened third is accentuated. Actually these 32 bars comprise two almost identical 16s; and at the end of the first sixteen (Bars 15 and 16) we have a 'break' (played by the banjo first time through and by the cornet and clarinet in a witty King Oliver-style mini-duet when the Theme is played again, led by the trombone, later).

The final bar of Theme A takes us through a modulating chord into the Key of Eb, in which Theme B is played. Twice through the sixteen bars (apparently both beginning with the chord sequence IV - IV - I - I) gives us a merry 32 bars. We then go straight back into Theme A (key of C again), with the trombone taking the lead. Then Theme B (in Eb) is re-visited. This is played through a couple of times with some boisterous, polyphonic ensemble, giving the piece a great ending. There is a neat Coda of just one bar.

Sorry to be a bit technical, but I think you can see how skilfully Shaye devises her music.

What a composition! It's just as well written and well played as those classics from the 1920s.

CHARLIE HALLORAN: TROMBONIST

One of the hardest-working and most versatile of the hugely-talented musicians I met during my visit to New Orleans in April 2015 was the trombone player Charlie Halloran. Charlie is one of the many young players who migrated to New Orleans - in his case from St. Louis - shortly after Hurricane Katrina.

Charlie had earlier studied at Webster University and went on to the Eastman School of Music in Rochester, New York.

It is not surprising that Charlie is in great demand. Is there any tune in any style that he can't play brilliantly? It seems not. I should mention that he's a pretty good singer, too.

During the four days of the official French Quarter Festival he played in at least nine concerts featuring various contrasting bands - *The Palmetto Bug Stompers*, *Tom Saunders and the Tomcats*, *Diablo's Horns*, *The Panorama Jazz Band*, *Steve Pistorius's Southern Syncopators*, *Cori Walters and the Universe Jazz Band*, *Orange Kellin's New Orleans Deluxe Orchestra*, and *Tim Laughlin's Band*. On top of these official Festival engagements, I saw him twice - in the evenings - playing with *The Shotgun Jazz Band* and with *Tuba Skinny*.

All that in four days. What stamina! What energy!

Charlie approaches his music in the same way that a great athlete approaches competition. He always aims to get a good sleep and does not stay out late when he doesn't have to. He makes a point of eating well.

Even on a day when there will be a lot of playing, he aims to be up by 9am to spend some time practising the trombone - 'warming up carefully' and 'playing long tones'. He carries in his kit a gel that he can apply to his lips in case of emergency. He says this helps prevent his lips from becoming swollen later in the day. (I noticed that Haruka Kikuchi, another great trombonist, occasionally applies vaseline to her lips during a performance.)

Yet, despite his massive talent, Charlie is such a modest and gentlemanly person, always friendly and willing to chat during his few spare moments. He loves his work but enjoys being a side-man rather a leader or star.

But listen to Charlie for yourself:

In this video, Charlie talks to us and gives a demonstration of some styles:

https://www.youtube.com/watch?v=da26kVkXyoY

Listen to a lovely gentle tune in 3/4 time with *The Panorama Jazz Band*: https://vimeo.com/124143248

You will need then to click the arrow button to run the video.

For Charlie playing *You Always Hurt the One You Love* with *The Shotgun Jazz Band*:

https://www.youtube.com/watch?v=5Rh52iL41gI

ALBANIE FALLETTA

I first came across the guitarist and singer Albanie Falletta in a delightful video, where, on the north bank of the Mississippi in New Orleans, with two string-playing friends, she performs *I'll See You in My Dreams*:

https://www.youtube.com/watch?v=d87WVpnegk4

I was immediately charmed.

And here is a wonderful April 2015 video filmed by the great *digitalalexa* of 'Albanie and her Fellas' playing in Royal Street, New Orleans. You could hardly have a better introduction to her:

https://www.youtube.com/watch?v=I1VNxXl6yhQ

With the help of YouTube, I found that Albanie often played in *The Thrift Set Orchestra* in Austin, Texas, with such fine musicians as Jonathan Doyle, Hal Smith, David Jellema and Westen Borghesi.

There is also a video of Albanie playing with Tuba Skinny at a French Quarter Festival.

So for months Albanie had been one of my favourites. Now imagine my joy when I visited New Orleans in April 2015 and spotted in Royal Street a young lady who looked exactly like Albanie. She had a guitar strapped to her back. 'Are you the famous Albanie?' I asked. 'Well, my name's Albanie,' she replied.

I found her just as sweet and charming as she appears in those videos. Albanie told me she came from Austin, where she started to teach herself to play the guitar at an early age. She has a good ear and usually has no trouble in working out the chords for a tune. She 'dropped out of high school' and took to busking and playing wherever she could. As you can see for yourself, she has mastered her instrument to a high degree and sings very pleasantly.

I later discovered Albanie is highly respected by the entire community of New Orleans musicians. Dividing her time between Austin and New Orleans, she gets to play in many different groups.

Now that she is internationally famous, we might think she would be satisfied with her achievements. But Albanie surprised me by saying she still hoped one day to go to college and study music academically. How modest these great young musicians on the New Orleans French Quarter scene always are! (Albanie told me the following year she was having to defer the idea of going to college as the streets of New Orleans had turned out to be a 'university' to her!)

My friend Bill Stock was the cameraman who made the video on the bank of the Mississippi.

THE SIDNEY STREET SHAKERS - AND A SPECIAL CD

An exciting discovery for me was *The Sidney Street Shakers*, a young band based in St. Louis, Missouri. In particular, important jazz-history research led to their first CD - *Laughing My Weary Blues Away*.

This band (basically an eight-piece) was formed in 2013 and is managed by multi-instrumentalist Kellie Everett. The musicians take pride in the contribution of St. Louis to early jazz history. They have set out to revive and recreate tunes composed and played by St. Louis musicians in the 1920s.

They claim the early history of jazz in St. Louis (as compared with that of New Orleans) has been relatively neglected. For example, quoting from their CD's liner notes: *'The greatness of St. Louis' music is due to St. Louis talent. Music didn't come to the city via the river; and that kind of thinking obscures the important contributions of St. Louis artists like Charlie Creath. Louis Armstrong was in the Waifs' Home in New Orleans when Creath was playing cornet in P. G. Lowrey's travelling show circulating early music ideas.'*

They also want to remind us that some of the earliest recordings were made in St. Louis and that mixed-race bands performed there surprisingly early in the history of jazz.

Kellie Everett must have done a phenomenal amount of work in researching the bands (most of whom left no recordings) and the jazz music they played. I guess you - like me - have never heard of the bands from whose work Kellie made her selection - *The Missourians, Harry's Happy Four, Dewey Jackson's Peacock Orchestra, Powell's Jazz Monarchs* and others. Kellie must have spent hundreds of hours transcribing the music from old recordings. Eventually she settled on a representative 15 tunes for inclusion on this CD.

You can find most of the 1920s performances of the originals on YouTube. Doing so helps you appreciate how meticulously the transcriptions have been made and how very closely these recreations follow the originals.

Accompanying the CD is a booklet largely written by historian Kevin Belford. Into eight small pages it crams a mass of information about the bands and the 15 tunes.

The CD has been really well recorded. The acoustics and balance are just right. You can hear every instrument clearly.

The music is played in a bright but respectful, accurate, tight, non-exhibitionist style by a group of fine musicians. They obviously work from Kellie's detailed transcriptions. The tunes invariably have arresting introductions and neat, clever codas. There is a clockwork, pulsating rhythm. Two-bar 'breaks' are well organised and constantly crop up (Jelly Roll Morton would have approved!). The trumpet - mostly stating the melody, is usually muted, and there is strong flavouring from the saxophones, including the bass sax which Kellie herself plays, Adrian Rollini-style. There are solos against stop chords; and you find 'Doo Wacka Doo' riffs here and there. Occasionally you may detect a kazoo, or even a comb-and-paper; and the voices of the musicians are built in to some of the arrangements - most noticeably in *Laughing Blues*, where an entire chorus of this 12-bar tune in F is filled with half the band laughing while a few keep the rhythm going - just as on the original 1926 recording by Powell's Jazz Monarchs.

The performances are peppered with short improvised 'solos' but these are always pretty, melodic and unpretentious rather than flashy - and that's just how I like them.

The great Chloe Feoranzo constantly provides flowing, lyrical decorations, whether on Clarinet or C Melody Sax, and she takes some sweet solo breaks. In *Hot Stuff*, Chloe shares a 32-bar theme with pianist Mary Ann Schulte (this is similar to what happens on the original 1929 recording of this tune by Oliver Cobb's Rhythm Kings). What a good player Mary is! She constantly provides the perfect underpinning of the music but she also shows herself very capable when given a chance to take a solo, as in *Blue Grass Blues*. This piece is extraordinary: it begins like something out of Chopin; and ends reminiscent of the final theme of 'Wolverine Blues'! To sample that track, you are welcome to listen to it in a YouTube I put together:

https://www.youtube.com/watch?v=yQqSaxpYMXM

Mary also has a pivotal rôle in *Market Street Stomp*. Chloe and Mary produce some fluent and pretty work on *East St. Louis Stomp*.

Kellie Everett herself plays so well throughout (bass and tenor sax) - showing that the bass sax can be a punchy alternative to a sousaphone or string bass and also that the instrument is capable of decent melody-making in its own right. The strings (Joe Park, Joey Glynn and - on some tracks - Jacob Alspach [he also plays trombone]) are always solid and have a chance to shine in *Blue Blood Blues*. The washboard and drums are played sympathetically by Ryan Koenig and Matt Meyer. Student percussionists could learn a lot by listening carefully to their discreet, sensitive support of the rest of the band. Kyle Butz is also very good on trombone: he plays on six of the tracks. Timothy John Muller, who, I gather, is also the on-stage music director of the band and helped Kellie considerably in preparing the scores, is - I'm proud to say - a fellow countryman of mine! He comes from Penrith in England. Tim leads with a mainly-muted trumpet, stating the melodies and producing variations very tastefully.

The tunes were all new to me. I was specially impressed by *Soap Suds* which seems to be a complex piece with a final theme that reminds me (harmonically) somewhat of *Bogalusa Strut*, though it's played in the unusual key of G. The little solos by Chloe and trombonist Kyle Butz are good examples of those pretty improvisations I mentioned.

Ozark Mountain Blues - an up-tempo number in Ab and anything but 'bluesy' - brings out powerful performances from all the band, and gets the CD off to a good start. And *Swinging The Swing* is a brisk, merry tune to add to our collection of tunes using the *Bill Bailey* chord sequence.

Hot Stuff is a tune we could all easily and profitably add to our repertoires - a medium-tempo straightforward AABA 32-bar in Eb, with a familiar chord progression.

The band takes its name from the Sidney Street that is a thoroughfare running west for over two miles from the Mississippi in St. Louis. The band used to rehearse in an apartment on that street when they first formed. On the evidence of Google Maps, it is a mostly leafy residential street with some attractive-looking houses.

You wish to obtain the CD? It's available at:
http://bigmuddyrecords.com/product/laugh-my-weary-blues-away/

By the way, Kellie Everett, the driving force behind the whole project, and who plays the saxes so well, has also been playing the banjo for twelve years. With two other members of the band, she belongs to the St. Louis Banjo Club. Trumpet-player T. J. Muller has also become a fine plectrum banjo player.

The jazz scene in St. Louis is growing, in combination with the local swing dancing revival.

ROBIN RAPUZZI

During my visits to New Orleans, I had the great pleasure of meeting Robin Rapuzzi. Robin is best known as the washboard player of Tuba Skinny.

Before he became a celebrated washboard player, Robin was a full-kit percussionist. He played the drum set at a young age and this led to participating in punk rock bands at high school. At that time, he also learned the guitar and harmonica. He enjoyed playing sea shanties, Woodie Guthrie tunes, and compositions of his own. He considered himself a 'folk musician' up to the time when he moved to New Orleans, where he took up the washboard specialism, joined Tuba Skinny and ...... the rest is history.

On some occasions, he told me, he has felt a bit limited in using the washboard only. For example, for such a tune as *New Orleans Bump*, he said that with the snare and Chinese tom-drum and china-crash cymbal he could access the depth and true texture that such a 'stompy' number deserved.

Since early 2015, he has returned to playing a full percussion set even in the streets. How has he managed to transport so much kit? The answer is that he hauls it around in a trailer attached to his bicycle. (He calls pedalling this load into the French Quarter his 'daily work-out'!)

Most of the New Orleans musicians use bicycles: it's almost impossible to park a car in the French Quarter.

I also had the pleasure of meeting Robin's lovely wife, Magda. She is Polish and is a highly-talented artist: she has produced some amazing work, often of dwellings in New Orleans but also sometimes combining mythical animal and human images with tremendous attention to detail. Her silk-screen prints are sold at

The Foundation Gallery in Royal Street and the Hall-Barnett Gallery on Chartres, as well as in other galleries. I realised a few days after meeting her that I had long admired Magda's work (through the internet) before discovering that she was married to Robin.

Although most fans think of Robin as a member of Tuba Skinny, he actually performs in several bands. He clearly enjoys the variety of work and is proud of them all. I think he was particularly pleased that I turned up to hear him with The Rhythm Wizards. On another day, I found Robin playing with The Hokum High Rollers.

There are hundreds of videos on YouTube of Robin playing with Tuba Skinny. But if you would like to watch one I made of them playing *Hilarity Rag* during this April 2016 visit, here it is:

https://www.youtube.com/watch?v=BvBxfc2jHb0

This is of historic interest because Robin told me it was a tune the Band had only just learned and this was its first public performance.

One of the interesting things Robin also told me is that it's not just the fans who enjoy the YouTube videos. He said many musicians - including himself - use them as learning tools. They analyse their own performances and consider what improvements could be made. He found it particularly interesting to spot how his own backing of, say, trombone solo choruses varied according to which trombonist he was playing with.

THE RHYTHM WIZARDS

Robin Rapuzzi is very proud of the work done in New Orleans by *The Rhythm Wizards,* one of the jazz bands in which he plays.

I can tell you this is a really good and interesting band, unusual because of its instrumentation and broad-minded repertoire. It is admirable that so many of the young musicians in New Orleans are introducing us to long-forgotten and unfamiliar tunes, including some with a Caribbean origin. This is so refreshing after all the *Bourbon Street Parades* and *When The Saints* and *Bill Baileys* that we constantly hear elsewhere.

The Rhythm Wizards were formed late in 2014, with Tomas Majcherski as leader. Some of the musicians had earlier played together in an experimental band called *The 4.99 Five-Piece* (a name based on fried chicken on sale in the market!); and some had played in *Steamboat Calypso* - the group led by Madeleine Reidy. Robin says they were very inspired by that group. In fact, Maddy was the singer on the first album *The Rhythm Wizards* produced.

Robin has great respect for the leadership provided by Tomas: he 'has done a ton of research for the group, especially when it comes to picking out the significant poly-rhythms that make Caribbean and jazz music so much fun to play'.

Robin kindly let me know *The Rhythm Wizards* intended to perform in Royal Street on 7 April 2016, while I was in town. So I made a point of being there.

Who are the members of the band? It's hard to give a definitive answer because the young New Orleans bands all seem to have a pool of players to draw upon. But the 'core' players seem to be:

Tomas Majcherski : Clarinet and Reeds

Robin Rapuzzi : Drums and Washboard

Jon Ramm : Trombone

Max Bien-Kahn : Guitar

Todd Burdick : banjo and tuba

Peter Olynciw : upright bass

Coleman Akin : Violin

Zayd Sifri : auxiliary percussion

Others who have played and recorded with them include:

Max Feldschuh : Vibraphone and Piano

Madeleine Reidy : vocals

You will notice that *The Rhythm Wizards* usually play without a trumpet and they have up to four musicians on stringed instruments. It is the clarinet that tends to lead on the melody. All these features help to make this a refreshingly distinctive traditional jazz band.

On its website, the Band claims to play 'Traditional Jazz and Pan-American Music from the Mississippi Delta to the Caribbean and beyond'. Such a repertoire also makes it rather special.

Yes, *The Rhythm Wizards* may be found playing a popular standard such as *Ice Cream*, or *St. Louis Blues*, or an elegant *Maple Leaf Rag*, but in the same programme you are also likely to hear that rarely-played number *St. Louis Tickle* and the rhythmic Caribbean-style *Petrol* or the sweetly melodic waltz-tempo *Tres Bemoles* (meaning 'Three Flats' - and it is indeed in the key of Eb). Or you may catch them playing *Black Rag*, which sounded to me like *Down Home Rag*. (I found later that *Down Home Rag* was composed in 1911, but that Papa Celestin's Tuxedo Orchestra was the first to record it - in 1925 - under the title *Black Rag*. I wonder why. To avoid paying dues?)

As you may infer, the variety of rhythms to be heard in a performance justifies their name as the 'Rhythm Wizards'.

One of their most popular numbers is *The History of Man. Codallo's Top Hatters Orchestra* of Trinidad recorded that tune in the 1930s, and *The Rhythm Wizards* are one of the few bands to be playing it today.

I made two videos of their performance in Royal Street on 7 April 2016. While filming, I slowly walked round the band, to get a good view of all of them in close-up. The result is that the sound quality is sometimes unbalanced but I hope the videos give a good idea of the kind of music the band plays and, incidentally, what busking is like for a musician on the streets of New Orleans.

In one of my videos, they are playing *The Cotton-Picker's Drag*. This tune was created by a string band of the 1930s - The Grinnell Giggers. View The Rhythm Wizards playing it:

https://www.youtube.com/watch?v=B6LYrMH7b-c

HARUKA THE PRODUCER

That great young Japanese trombone player Haruka Kikuchi was very proud at the end of 2016. Why? Because, although she had played on many recordings and with the best bands, she had now - for the first time - become the Producer of a fine new recording; and I think she intended it to be the first of a series. She called it JAPAN: NEW ORLEANS COLLECTION SERIES Volume One.

The music was very well recorded, with fine acoustics and balance. Haruka's band comprises five musicians and has a distinctive brassy sound, with trumpet, sousaphone and trombone and no reeds. On trumpet is Naho Ishimura, yet another brilliant young Japanese musician, whose playing is nimble and lyrical. Steven Glenn makes a solid and melodic contribution on sousaphone; and who better to provide the chords and drumming than Albanie Falletta (guitar) and the highly-experienced Gerald French on drums (and vocals)? To sample the sounds, go here:

http://harombone.bandcamp.com/album/japan-new-orleans-collection-series-vol-1

You will even hear the vocals to *Struttin' With Some Barbecue* and *Muskrat Ramble*. That's something that doesn't often happen!

When I met Haruka for the first time, in 2015, she was playing with *The Shotgun Jazz Band*, as well as *Kermit Ruffins and the BBQ Swingers* and *The Swamp Donkeys*. She toured with *The Swamp Donkeys* in England, Scotland, France, Holland and Spain during July and August 2015. The following year, as well as touring in Japan, she became more independent: she played with even more bands but also started a band of her own. Her diary is so full: it seems to me that she averages seven gigs a week - sometimes with seven different bands!

Haruka started learning to play the piano, violin and cornet from an early age. But when she was 15 she was bowled over by discovering the early recordings of New Orleans jazz. She decided the 'tailgate trombone' was for her, her hero being Kid Ory. She studied at Tokyo University of the Arts, graduating in 2010 with a degree in Music Science.

DAVID JELLEMA

I first noticed and admired the cornet player David Jellema in 2014, when on YouTube I discovered videos of *The Thrift Set Orchestra*, which is based in Austin, Texas. David was playing some fine music in the company of other outstanding musicians - among them, Albanie Falletta, Westen Borghesi and Jonathan Doyle. If you don't know this group, you may sample one of their performances here:

https://www.youtube.com/watch?v=1GhiQdoXDF0

But I didn't meet David until 20 October 2016 when, during a very brief visit to New Orleans, I literally bumped into him. I pushed open the door to the Yuki Izakaya Bar in Frenchmen Street, and David was immediately on the other side. He was guesting in Haruka Kikuchi's Band.

During the interval, David kindly and generously joined me for a very interesting chat.

In particular we discussed how he goes about mastering tunes and improvising upon them. He felt that, although it is obviously crucial to know the tune's melody and its chords, it becomes more important to internalize those elements (relegating them to the subconscious through repetition and practice - to the point where you would be able to play the song even in an unfamiliar key). With the music thus internalized, the conscious mind can be free to engage with the immediate demands of the performance in the present, i.e., listening and responding to the other musicians, making split-second choices within a solo, etc.

Beyond mastering the scales and arpeggios of chord shapes and inversions in all keys, David said, what is most important in developing jazz improvisational language, style, and a personal voice is to study many masters (by copious listening, transcribing, and copying their solos and licks) in order to let their influence percolate into your playing as you mature into your own voice.

The music you most love will help inform and shape your first steps towards developing your own improvisational style. In his own case, he said the most important master had been Bix Beiderbecke.

I was not surprised. In his fluency, creativity, attack, tone and technique, David's playing always reminds me of Bix.

But here's something astonishing. David plays a cornet that is over 120 years old; and he still gets a beautiful tone from it. The cornet is an 1893 English Besson, a vintage 'Prototype' (serial number 48XXX). David knows that F. Besson was at the time located at 198, Euston Road, London; and that the instruments were distributed in the USA by Carl Fischer of New York. David bought this cornet from an antique store in Annapolis, Maryland, in the 1990s. As the US Naval Academy is based in Annapolis, David surmises that the instrument may originally have been played by someone in the Navy band.

After a few years, David passed the cornet on to his friend Dave Sager, a jazz trombone player in the DC area. Mr. Sager spent a deal of money in having it brought back to a pristine condition. Since about 2011, it has been back in the hands of David Jellema.

THE WORLD'S BEST FRONT LINE

I remember seeing in a jazz magazine about thirty years ago a photograph with the caption 'The World's Best Front Line'.

It was a picture taken in a New Orleans bar and showed a trumpet player, with a clarinettist and a trombonist on either side of him, playing their hearts out and obviously pleasing the journalist or photographer.

I was reminded of this when it occurred to me that the World's Best Front Line Award for musicians active *today* could well go to Jonathan Doyle (clarinet), Shaye Cohn (cornet) and Barnabus Jones (trombone). When those three together, there is no matching them for rapport, teamwork and musical brilliance.

How thrilling they can make any tune sound, even just a basic 12-bar, as in this recent video put up on YouTube by the generous *digitalalexa*, with Erika Lewis producing a terrific vocal as ever:

https://www.youtube.com/watch?v=ZJe0oYeXErk

Interestingly, of course, these musicians rarely appear literally as a 'front line' - preferring, when space allows, for their band to be spread out in a semi-circle, so that all the players can see each other and the audience can see all the musicians. It is also easier for signals to be given by the leader. I wish more bands would adopt this formation.

And may I mention another thrilling 'front line' that I had the privilege of filming. It was *The Shotgun Jazz Band*'s Haruka Kikuchi (trombone), Marla Dixon (trumpet) and James Evans (reeds). Try this performance, in which they play 'Climax Rag':

https://www.youtube.com/watch?v=h77s41Q0w5o

THE GENTILLY STOMPERS

One of the best traditional jazz bands to appear in 2016 (even though it was formed only at the beginning of that year) was *The Gentilly Stompers*. The band also recorded its first CD (expected to be called 'Thanks A Million!' and last heard of going through its pre-release processing).

I found them playing at Bamboula's in Frenchmen Street. And a very enjoyable session it was. The Band played mainly the standard repertoire in good but uncomplicated arrangements. The teamwork and musicianship were outstanding.

The Band had been formed by yet another great lady trumpet-player - Catie Rodgers. Her own playing is first-class and she is a good leader - giving clear directions and encouraging all members of the band to show what they can do.

I managed to have a few words with Catie. She told me she studied Music at the local University of New Orleans, specialising in trumpet playing. She is a fine classical trumpet player. But classical trumpet players do not always make good traditional jazz players. Catie is an exception. She is an outstanding player in the New Orleans jazz idiom, whether stating a melody with minimal decoration, or improvising a solo chorus with great technical proficiency.

Catie told me she is 'going for clarity and soul'. One of her main influences was the cornet player Connie Jones, who had recently retired. She told me 'His lines and feeling really can't be beat'. She said her policy had been to recruit musicians who are sharp, sensitive listeners and really good, fun people. 'I believe that creates an inviting dynamic, and a positive environment to hang in.

I'm always looking for more inspiration, whether it be recordings, old or new, or in my peers as we grow and change together'.

Her core players at July 2016 were: Haruka Kikuchi (trombone), Chloe Feoranzo (reeds), Alex Belhaj (guitar), Miles Lyons (tuba) and Sean Clark (drums).

But how did Catie come to be leader of a band called *The Gentilly Stompers*?

While still a student (in about 2012), she started gigging in the City. She did quite a bit of deputising for absent trumpet players. As they were often the band leaders, she found herself in both a directing as well as a deputising role. Soon people began to suggest that she should officially become a band-leader and run a band of her own.

Why call it *The Gentilly Stompers*? It is named after Gentilly, the New Orleans suburb about four miles north of the French Quarter. Gentilly is on the south side of Lake Pontchartrain and it is also where The University of New Orleans is situated.

How has Catie mastered the art of playing the trumpet so well? By putting in many years of hard work, I am sure. But she also told me the secret lies in loving the instrument. 'I have great respect for the trumpet and I think that's very important.'

I made a video of the band playing *Honeysuckle Rose*. Unfortunately, because of the conditions in the bar, the lighting and sound qualities are far from perfect, but I hope it will give you some idea of how good this band really is. Go to:

https://www.youtube.com/watch?v=BE7Ww7o_06o

By the summer of 2016, Catie decided to head to Kansas City to pursue yet higher classical trumpet musical studies at the University of Missouri. That was sad for the fans. She was missed in New Orleans. However, she was back in the City playing some gigs with the band at the end of December 2016, presumably during her university vacation. And in March 2017 she returned 'permanently' to the City. I am sure we all wish her well - and hope she will keep the band going.

SUN LANE LTD. NEW ORLEANS JAZZ BAND

The Sun Lane Ltd. New Orleans Jazz Band comprises seven pretty old boys based in Aachen, Germany. For me they are a new discovery – recommended to me by an Australian friend. He said he would be happy listening to this band for hours on end. I can understand that.

I have never seen the band in person but there are plentiful good examples of their work on YouTube. I like them. The way they arrange their tunes is pretty much the same as in 95% of the bands operating all over Europe, Australasia and America - straightforward statements of the themes, followed by solo choruses until the out-chorus. But what I like particularly is the way they play tastefully and unpretentiously, with real delicacy and restraint (even in the rhythm section) and no sense of strain. The teamwork is good. After many years of working together, they have a very 'tight' sound. These chaps really *listen* to each other.

From its website, I learn this is a busy band, with plenty of bookings in Cologne. *The Sun Lane Ltd. New Orleans Jazz Band* was founded as long ago as 1977, at The University of Aachen. Over the years, they have played at festivals throughout Europe; and the band has been to New Orleans more than once - giving concerts there. Possibly their proudest moment came when they were booked to play the evening performance at Preservation Hall on 30 April, 2002.

Not surprisingly, the band has built up a large repertoire and has made several CDs.

How about sampling this fine band for yourself? To hear them play *Bugle Boy March*:

https://www.youtube.com/watch?v=nlEV9gm8sl4

And here is *Postman's Lament*:

https://www.youtube.com/watch?v=JgQoTuobwv8

As ever, we have to be grateful to video-makers who bring such fine things to our computer screens. In this case: thank you, Uli van Royen.

THE HOKUM HIGH ROLLERS

On the streets of New Orleans, there are now several fine young 'string bands'. It is not just standard traditional jazz bands that have flourished there in the last ten years.

These groups are direct descendants of the string and jug bands from the 1930s, such as *The Dixieland Jug Blowers*, *The South Street Trio*, *The State Street Boys*, *The Dallas String Band*, *The Mississippi Sheiks*, *The Memphis Jug Band*, *The Grinnell Giggers*, *The Mississippi Mud Steppers*, *Bo Carter's Bands*, *King David's Jug Band*, who have inspired them and from whom they derive much of their repertoire. The music of string bands also of course fed directly into the 'country' and 'bluegrass' genres.

One of the best of today's bands is *The Hokum High Rollers*. There are plenty of good videos of them on YouTube. If you haven't yet watched it, try this one as an example of their brilliance and virtuosity:

https://www.youtube.com/watch?v=lkb6-3CLkhU

I was thrilled to come across them busking in Royal Street during my April 2016 visit to New Orleans. Listening and watching from close quarters showed me they work hard, take their playing very seriously and have attained the highest technical standard of musicianship. You can watch it here:

https://www.youtube.com/watch?v=1fbLWQR-tRY

'But is this strictly traditional jazz?' you ask. Yes, though it is played by some instruments you don't find in conventional bands. The musicians are comfortable playing in a string band or in a stock jazz band. Two of *The Hokum High Rollers* in my video are also members of *Tuba Skinny*. And the tune they are playing -

Michigander Blues - has become popular with many jazz bands since *Tuba Skinny* started playing it a few years ago.

THE SCENE IN NEW ORLEANS

On my brief visits to New Orleans in 2015 and 2016, I had the privilege of conversations with several of the musicians I had previously seen and admired only on YouTube; and I listened to some of the great bands playing in the bars and clubs (such as *The Spotted Cat* and *The DBA* and *The Maison*).

They tend to live in rented shotgun houses just outside the French Quarter. Some of them are near enough to walk to work. But many use bicycles, often fitted with trailers, to take themselves and their kit to the spot where they will play.

They work long and hard. Typically, guitarist Shine Delphi spent a day busking with *Yes Ma'am* from 11am until 2pm; and then had a gig from 3pm until 5pm, and ended with another gig at Buffa's from 11pm until 1am. And that was on his birthday!

You sometimes pass a band playing for tips at a certain spot and then - when you return five hours later - you find they are still there and still playing. What stamina they have! The famous Doreen Ketchens, for example, plays very long sessions in Royal Street.

Musical standards are so high. For example, I noticed street musicians have no problem playing terrific improvised 32-bar solo choruses even when they have a singer who chooses to sing in an 'awkward' key. Pretty well any of the musicians busking on Royal Street would be instant stars on the jazz scene here in England. But in England they would not make a living, whereas in New Orleans the tips from tourists give them just enough to live on.

There are now so many street musicians in New Orleans that competition for attention and for tips has become a problem. In Royal Street (the main location for buskers), you may be brilliantly singing songs accompanied by your own guitar, but there will be a five-piece band only 100 yards to your right and a solo classical violinist 100 yards to your left. So it's not easy to hold the attention of passers-by.

In addition, the streets are full of other 'entertainers' - the human statues, tap-dancers, the man who types instant poetry, the sword swallower, the magician, the exhibitionists (often vulgar) who expect tips just for posing in outrageous costumes, and so on.

I was told independently by two musicians (so it is surely true) that, if you want to play in a prime spot from 11a.m. (when music is allowed), you need some member of your band to man that position from 11p.m. the night before. All through the night, someone must be on the spot to hold it. Sometimes members of a band do this in 'shifts', with one arriving at 2a.m. to relieve the musician on duty since 11 pm., and so on. How can they be fit to play after such a night? It's tough; and for this reason some who are now being offered decent gigs in the bars have decided not to play on the streets any more.

Of course there are other spots (such as on the Walk along the north bank of the Mississippi) where you could set up and play, but far fewer people pass by there.

When you talk to the musicians, it's not easy to get some of them to be serious on the subject of their talents. They constantly joke and belittle themselves. But some, notably Tommy Sancton, Ben Polcer, Charlie Halloran and John Dixon, were happy to chat about the technicalities of the music. What impressed me was how seriously they take it and how hard they work and practise. On rare days when there is no gig, they still insist on the need to practise for a couple of hours. As one said, 'It's like being an iceberg. The public sees the little bit above the water; but there's a huge amount of hard work that goes on underneath the surface'.

I asked how important it was for trumpet, clarinet and trombone players to know the chord progression of a particular tune. To my surprise, they all considered it essential. Of course, they pointed out that - when you have played a tune many times - the chord sequence is 'in your fingers' and instinctive, so you no longer consciously think of it; but you must learn it in the first place.

Did they reach a point at which they had no need to learn any more tunes? Definitely not. The joy of mastering new tunes goes on and on. Ben Polcer - who as a young music graduate was among the first to migrate to New Orleans - is a brilliant player of both the piano and the trumpet. He has been one of the most important influential figures on the New Orleans scene since Hurricane Katrina. Yet he is still learning new tunes. He told me he can usually pick up a tune of the more 'straightforward' kind after hearing it a couple of times, especially if he recognizes familiar chord sequences within it.

One of the most exciting musicians on the current New Orleans scene is Aurora Nealand, who plays in various contrasting styles with different bands, some of which she leads. Typical of the sort of thing Aurora does was this: her band started to play *Dans Les Rues d'Antibes* with its usual brisk up-tempo Introduction. Then they suddenly stopped and switched to a weird almost dirge-like bit of (what seemed to me) free-style jazz. It was fun and went on for about a minute. Then they bounced back into *Dans Les Rues* and performed it in the conventional way, with some sensationally good solo choruses. Playful treatments such as that seem to be something Aurora is very keen to experiment with.

154

Aurora - like many of the others - went to New Orleans intending to stay for about six months, mainly working at composing. But the culture soon got into her blood. Inspired by *The Preservation Hall Band* in her childhood, she had always loved traditional jazz. So she started to study it more deeply and soon found herself constantly playing on the streets - with various bands.

She is now one of the most brilliant and versatile reed players and band-leaders in the world. Aurora told me there is something very special about playing with bands in New Orleans. She said the technical standard of traditional jazz musicians in New York is extremely high; and yet compared with New York (where incidentally some of the New Orleans musicians spend a month or two in the summer), she found there was something more 'relaxed' and less cerebral about the music in New Orleans. This quality is hard to define; but it's there all right.

One of the fascinating things about being in the French Quarter of New Orleans is that you can't walk more than a hundred yards down Royal Street or Bourbon Street without seeing musicians coming to or returning from performances on the streets or in the bars and clubs.

It is virtually impossible to take a car into the French Quarter, so most of them have found enterprising ways of transporting even the bulkiest instruments and equipment. The bicycle is a very important tool in the kit of most musicians. Trailers are often fitted. Those fortunate enough to live close by may be able to walk to work, carrying their instruments. One such is the gentleman who regularly walks into Jackson Square with his sousaphone round his neck.

THE PALMETTO BUG STOMPERS

One of the best bands I heard at The French Quarter Festival in New Orleans during April 2016 was *The Palmetto Bug Stompers*. I caught their performance on the French Market Stage.

I had never seen the band in person before, even though I was aware they had been in existence for at least fifteen years and that there were many good videos of them on YouTube.

Why did I think they were so good? Begin with their rhythm section, which pulsates and drives in the best New Orleans tradition, without ever being too loud. They do not use a drum kit: instead, a washboard, guitar and bass work together as one man. And there is equally good taste in the 'front line' where the musicians listen well to each other, and interweave their patterns with beauty and subtlety. The tone is set by Will Smith on trumpet, who is not one of those exhibitionist trumpet-players who scream around the high notes just for the sake of it. Instead, he shows respect for the melodies and the soul of the music. So the band plays with good taste, and yet builds up excitement in a controlled way.

Where I stood, at the side of the band and in the middle of a large, noisy, jostling crowd, it was very difficult to take a video. I tried; and the result may be seen on YouTube here:

https://www.youtube.com/watch?v=W4wvXM4awy4

One of the problems with the crowded Festival events is that it is sometimes more difficult to enjoy the bands than when they are playing in smaller, more intimate venues, where audience comfort and acoustics are better. But I hope this video will also give you some sense of the atmosphere at the annual Festival.

May I recommend this band to you? Watch some more of their YouTube videos. And, if you ever get the chance, aim to see them.

MEET DIZZY – WHAT A GAL!

In 2013, on YouTube, I first spotted Dizzy, playing with *Yes Ma'am*, the string band, and also deputising for Robin Rapuzzi with *Tuba Skinny*. I was watching a young lady who was not only a great washboard player but also the world's most beautiful musician.

When I travelled the 4,500 miles from my home to New Orleans for the French Quarter Festival in April 2015, I was disappointed that I did not come across Dizzy, though I heard later that she had been busking in the streets when I was there.

However, visiting again in April 2016, I found *Yes Ma'am* playing in The French Market. They were brilliant - even better in person than in their many YouTube videos.

I had a lovely chat with Dizzy. As I had expected, she turned out to be a very articulate, good-humoured and warm-hearted person.

This young lady had been settled in New Orleans for several years. She plays sublimely and prolifically with a number of bands. Mostly, she is with *Yes Ma'am*.

If you think playing the washboard is easy, you are wrong. It takes some doing to maintain the strict tempo and to decorate properly the music being played by the rest of your group. You have to know the tunes really well, especially to be aware of 'breaks' and rhythmic changes. It's hard work on the fingers and wrists, too. You need a lot of energy.

Dizzy is a brilliant player of the washboard. My favourite video of her is this one:

https://www.youtube.com/watch?v=nEmU3E8rras

Incidentally, that great song - *Caffeine* - was composed by the gentleman singing it - Aaron Gunn.

But if you would like to see Dizzy playing in a more conventional traditional jazz band, here's one of her in Mexico with *Tuba Skinny*. Watch out for her enjoying a solo chorus at 2 minutes 41 seconds:

https://www.youtube.com/watch?v=gCAWIBbcGJA

Dizzy has a Turkish background and speaks both English and Turkish fluently. As a child she had piano lessons and also started to play the saxophone. (She told me she is still playing the piano quite a lot.) She went on to be a high-flying graduate in English and American Literature and Creative Writing at New York University. Then in 2009 she chose to go to New Orleans to 'collect material' to write about. It seems she is still collecting it!

What she obviously did collect was washboards and she chose this happy if unconventional busking life-style. I made a video of her playing in *Yes Ma'am* on 7 April 2016 - the date when at last I met her. I hope you will watch it:

https://www.youtube.com/watch?v=Owz7P3l9joI

Since June 2016, Dizzy has also been the percussionist of the great all-ladies band formed by Shaye Cohn and called *The Shake 'Em Up Jazz Band*.

Early in 2017 she took up playing a full percussion kit and became the drummer in the band *Max and the Martians*.

THE HALFWAY HOUSE ORCHESTRA

Among the most obvious New Orleans bands from the early days whose work we should study were those of Sam Morgan and Armand Piron. The recordings they made are invaluable sources of inspiration and information to all of us who wish to perpetuate the music.

But there was another very good recording band in New Orleans at that time. This was *The Halfway House Orchestra*, which flourished from 1923 until 1928.

Its leader was Albert 'Abbie' Brunies. The rest of the players included (over the years) Leon Roppolo, Charles Cordilla, Joe Loyacano and Sidney Arodin (reeds), Bill Eastwood and Angelo Palmisano (banjo), Mickey Marcour, Bill Whitmore and Glyn Lea 'Red' Long (piano), Deacon Loyacano, Johnny Saba (vocals), Chink Martin (bass and tuba) and Bud Loyacano (string bass), Leo Adde, Emmett Rogers and Monk Hazel (drums - Hazel also played cornet and mellophone), and Merritt Brunies (valve trombone).

How did this jazz band get its name? It played at The Halfway House Dance Hall, in City Park Avenue, two miles north of the New Orleans City Centre - *half-way* to the Lake (Pontchartrain). The dance hall was popular because it provided both good food and fine bands. Albert 'Abbie' Brunies was director of the resident band for seven years.

This historic building ceased being a venue in about 1930 and was eventually demolished in 2010, when it was found to be in too poor a condition to renovate, even though there had been support for the idea of turning it into a jazz museum.

Led by 'Abbie' Brunies, *The Halfway House Orchestra* recorded 22 tunes between 1925 and 1928 - 18 of them for Columbia. A few of these were standards (*Squeeze Me*, *Let Me Call You Sweetheart*, *Maple Leaf Rag* - the last one played perhaps too fast, though you can't normally say that of this band); but more than half the tunes were original compositions by members of the band - especially Brunies, Long and Eastwood.

A good place to start, if you wish to sample this band, is *Baratari*, composed by the band's Bill Eastwood and Leo Adde:

https://www.youtube.com/watch?v=6LoGUErBAdQ

It is a melodic and dance-able 32-bar [16 + 16] structure in Bb, with a simple chord sequence and what sounds like a Gb chord (for a bit of surprise colouring) on bars 25 and 26. It allows for breaks (on the chord of F7) in Bars 15 and 16; and there is a Verse which has echoes of the first theme of *Wolverine Blues*. The performance is altogether pleasant and there are no prima donnas among the musicians.

And their *Pussy Cat Rag* (composed by Brunies, Cordilla and Marcour) is a simple enough piece that really romps along, with some subtle syncopation.

It Belongs to You (by Brunies and Lea) is one of those 16-bar tunes allowing for plenty of two-bar breaks (almost identical to *If It Don't Fit, Don't Force It* and *How Come You Do Me Like You Do, Do, Do?*). Such tunes were very fashionable at the time and are still easy - and fun - to play.

This band played for dancers and it shows. They were really good at giving the dancers what they wanted. You can sense it in all these recordings.

For me, the most appealing is *New Orleans Shuffle*, composed by their pianist Bill Whitmore. It opens with a very unusual 10-bar 'oriental' introduction. Then comes a bouncing 32-bar [16 + 16] Verse, ending on Ab7, which leads perfectly into the 32-bar Main

Theme (very swingy and melodic) in Db. Next comes a key change! The clarinet plays the theme in Bb. After this we transition back to Db for the cornet to play the theme. Finally, we have the full ensemble playing an out-chorus vigorously reminiscent of the King Oliver Band in which Louis Armstrong played second cornet (there's even a *Snake Rag*-style break on the chord of Ab7 in Bars 15-16!). Listen to the performance:

https://www.youtube.com/watch?v=AS0unZ0B6qI

The Halfway House Orchestra seems to have had a preference for very sing-able tunes interpreted in uncomplicated and neat, unpretentious arrangements, with pleasant interplay between cornet and reeds and a steady pulse provided with restraint by the rhythm section.

So it's a band worth noting - playing its music in a relaxed and melodic way that many of us still consider just right for traditional jazz.

TODD BURDICK AND BARNABUS JONES

An American friend – Lou – sent me this message:

I have commented on a few members of Tuba Skinny, but I have to mention Barnabus. Of course I listened to the traditional recorded dixieland growing up. But we spent every weekend during my college days at a local jazz place. We listened to the "Dixiecrats", a great band consisting of piano, tenor sax, trumpet, clarinet, string bass and drums. The tenor and sax played with Cab Calloway and the clarinet played with Louis Armstrong in the early days in NOLA. So I was pretty used to a band without a trombone, and never gave the instrument much thought. As a matter of fact, we thought of our taste in dixieland as rather elite....no tuba, no banjo, strictly "Chicago Style".

Tuba Skinny has totally changed my thinking on the subject, which is a lengthy lead-in to Barnabus.

I suspect that he, Shaye and Todd go back to their earliest days together and that they have not only a strong personal relationship, but are attuned to one another musically. Barnabus is such a strong player. He's always where he should be, whether it's lead or support. I still find it hard to believe that he just picked up a horn and taught himself. He certainly plays like he has a deep musical background. The same thing seems true of Todd. He's so gentle that at times he sounds like a string bass, and he's so important as part of TS's rhythm section.

I am so pleased Lou pays this tribute to Barnabus and Todd.

Tuba Skinny fans (including myself) are so seduced by the amazing talents of the ladies - Shaye and Erika - that we don't give sufficient credit to the other players - especially Todd, who goes unnoticed by most people while never putting a foot wrong in the engine room of the band.

Sometimes, when listening to a tune played by Tuba Skinny, I deliberately focus my attention on ONE instrument. It is a great way to appreciate the magic of this band. I am invariably amazed at how that one instrument contributes to the overall structure. In the case of Barnabus, Lou is so right about his strengths, whether leading on the melody or supporting other players. And Todd has an uncanny ability to find the perfect bass line, no matter how complicated the piece. Maybe the fact that both these men are also banjo players - and therefore understand chord sequences - helps a little. What great musicians they both are!

THE EXTRA CRISPY BRASS BAND

I discovered *The Extra Crispy Brass Band* during explorations on YouTube.

I enjoyed what I heard. And a good thing about this band is that its members are relatively *young*.

I have since found out that the band was formed in 2011 and is based in Milwaukee, Wisconsin. That's more than 1000 miles north of New Orleans; or, to put it another way, it's on the west shore of Lake Michigan, about 90 miles north of Chicago.

The Extra Crispy Brass Band aims to play in the tradition of such New Orleans brass bands as *The Dirty Dozen* and *The Olympia*. Indeed, the band was founded and is led by trombonist Gregory Cramer, who used to live in New Orleans.

As is common practice with brass bands, there are no chord players (banjo or guitar) but they double up with two trumpets, two trombones and have at least one saxophone. The percussion (two players) is the essential department. Such bands of course usually have as their basis great rhythms laid down by the drummers and sousaphone, generating pulsating riffy excitement. This band certainly works that way.

For a well-made video to give you some idea of their appearance and sound, here them play *Royal Garden Blues*:

https://www.youtube.com/watch?v=ByiHMFdk1AY

Maybe this will encourage you to explore other videos of them.

JAZZ IN JAPAN

May I suggest you watch this delightful video made by young traditional jazz musicians in Japan? It shows vividly how the music is thriving in that country and also how it can be played with joy. Go to this YouTube:

https://www.youtube.com/watch?v=QDRQnYHuUuk

If I have understood correctly, the Band is *The Khachaturian Jazz Band* (The Khacha Band, for short) and the players are Tomomitsu Maruyama (leader, banjo and vocals), Naho Ishimura (trumpet and tambourine), Kensuke Shintani (clarinet), Hishinuma Naoki (tuba), and Tomohiko Miwa (percussion).

I have never been to Japan and I know very little about traditional jazz in that country. But we all know there has long been - albeit on a small scale - a strong tradition of New Orleans-style jazz played particularly in Tokyo and Osaka. So let me state what I can.

There seem to have been Japanese musicians even before World War II who were influenced by American dance band and early jazz music. For example, listen to this recording of *Tiger Rag*:

https://www.youtube.com/watch?v=HbFtbidDNyE

Later, it seems that a group of enthusiastic young musicians from about 1955 were influenced by the New Orleans Jazz Revival, and notably by such musicians as George Lewis, Jim Robinson and Bunk Johnson. The Band called *The New Orleans Rascals* was formed in 1961. And it still performs today, mainly, I think, in Osaka. Those young musicians started making records early in their career. And they enjoyed a terrific boost when George Lewis visited Japan with his band in 1963.

The visit by George Lewis was a big sensation at the time, seminal and influential. In fact, its legacy is still strong. I think I am right in saying there are many musicians in Japan today who still feel that the ONLY correct way to play the music is in the style of George Lewis.

I remember that in about 1980 a friend who was crazy about The New Orleans Rascals gave me a cassette tape of their recordings. They certainly were very good, sounding much like a George Lewis band and playing his repertoire. Over the years, The New Orleans Rascals have often played at festivals abroad and, in their turn, they have hosted many fine guest performers from other parts of the world. My friend David Withers in New Zealand told me the late Mike Durham, best known as the leader of The West Jesmond Rhythm Kings, lived in Japan in the 1980s, playing with a band called *The Kobe Stompers*.

Rhoichi Kawai (devotedly a disciple of George Lewis) has not only been the great clarinet player of The New Orleans Rascals; he also formed a club in 1958 – The Waseda University New Orleans Jazz Club – and it still exists today. Waseda University is in Tokyo. In fact Rhoichi Kawai was the dominant figure in Japanese traditional jazz for decades. He is considered a great pioneer and is held in respect even by the much younger generation of musicians.

Members of the Club included Mari Watanabe, the fine pianist who moved to New Orleans about twenty years ago, and still plays there at Preservation Hall and The Palm Court Café. She is married to Roger Lewis, who plays the sax with The Tremé Brass Band and the Dirty Dozen Brass Band.

Another club member was the great pianist Natsuko Furukawa, whose brilliance may be appreciated in many videos. She now lives in Kawasaki where she runs the band *Soul Food*

167

Café, with her husband playing the saxophone. They occasionally visit New Orleans. You can watch her in storming action in this video:

https://www.youtube.com/watch?v=QWJlyrV1Ijw

And how about sampling a performance of *The Old Rugged Cross* by The New Orleans Rascals in 1991, with leader Rhoichi Kawai on clarinet? Here it is:

https://www.youtube.com/watch?v=zeQosPqhUa8

Yoshio Toyama (trumpet), who has frequently visited New Orleans to play, was also a member. In more recent years, Kensuke Shintani (clarinet), Haruka Kikuchi (trombone) and Makiko Tamura (clarinet) were members. Another important former club member is Hiro Kodaira. He lived in New Orleans for many years and played the banjo in Jackson Square. Many street musicians there still remember him; but he returned to Japan after Hurricane Katrina.

It has been impossible for Japanese traditional jazz musicians to make a full-time living from the music. Traditional jazz is not quite popular enough among the general public – a situation common in most countries. Rhoichi Kawai himself, for example, had a day job running a jewellery store.

There seem to be quite a few bands currently on the scene. For example, (playing in Tokyo) The New Orleans Jazz Hounds include several young musicians. I know that the work of Makiko Tamura – the superb young lady clarinet player – is greatly admired You can find examples of her playing on YouTube.

The leader of The New Orleans Jazz Hounds is Mikio Shoji (piano), who was mostly inspired by the late Danny Barker.

And there is Nobu Ozaki, the bassist with John Boutté, who seems to be the only Japanese traditional jazz person who didn't join the Waseda University New Orleans Jazz Club! He preferred to move young to New Orleans.

Kensuke Shintani (already mentioned) is a superb clarinet player. Also in Tokyo is Tomomitsu Maruyama who plays the banjo. You saw both these men in the video I recommended at the top of this article. Haruka Kikuchi considers Tomomitsu the best traditional banjo player in the world.

Some of the younger Japanese musicians, such as Haruka Kikuchi, are by no means stuck in the past but are absorbing the many influences that have infiltrated traditional jazz in New Orleans itself during recent years. I am referring to Baltic brass band music, Caribbean rhythms and calypsos, and even Mardi Gras Indian 'funky' music. Haruka, the great trombonist, set up home in New Orleans at the end of 2013, and has played with pretty well all the great bands there, even forming one herself, and she has happily toured as a member of the Mardi Gras Indian Funk Band called *Cha Wa*. Haruka told me she wants to be a bridge to the next generation. She thinks the jazz culture she has found in New Orleans is slightly different from the one she left in Tokyo. She is glad she has settled in New Orleans because she says 'I have to learn and study many things here, and want to play good music. Just good music with everybody (no matter where they are from!).'

Finally, have a look at a distinctive Japanese group playing *In The Mood* and *The Kentucky Waltz*. Robert Wendorf (resident in Japan) drew it to my attention.

https://www.youtube.com/watch?v=NqVTs--fJDo

SECTION 4: THE LEGACY

Our music has a long and massive history. Recordings of it have been made for a hundred years. I want to tell you about just a few of the bands and musicians from the past whose work has particularly impressed me.

THE OLDEST SURVIVING VENUE

Let me tell you about a truly legendary building. It is the oldest surviving venue in the world in which jazz was played in the earliest years of its development; and traditional jazz is again being played there today. I'm referring to the The Dew Drop Dance and Social Hall, which is situated at 430 Lamarque Street in Old Mandeville, Louisiana. Lamarque Street is to this day a quiet sparsely-populated, leafy, narrow road.

I set foot in The Dew Drop Hall in April 2015, when I was in New Orleans for the French Quarter Festival.

But the story begins on 5 May 1885, when local African Americans created *The Dew Drop Social and Benevolent Association* - aiming to provide help to the sick and the needy.

The Association built the hall from cypress timber nine years later - and opened it in 1895. Its foundations were simple brick piers (a wise choice for flood protection). The pier at the front on the left still bears the original inscription (now barely legible).

It commemorates the founding of the Dew Drop Social and Benevolent Society No. 2 of Mandeville on May 5th, 1885, and the construction of the building in 1895, along with the names of the building committee.

The walls were covered with weather-boards at the front, and batten on the sides and rear; and they were originally painted green. The carpenters created the large wooden double-door at the front gable end, and a smaller door on the right at the back. There was an open beam ceiling. It was essentially a one-room structure, available for meetings, celebrations, vaudeville, dances and so on. It became the centre of social life.

The dais (mainly used as a bandstand) at the far end was typical of the time - with a wooden banister front opening in two places for the steps. The hall was built without electricity - or plumbing - or even glass: the 'windows' were simply openings measuring 6 feet high by 4 feet wide. They were normally covered by wooden shutters. These windows must have helped keep the band and audience cool on humid evenings.

But where exactly is it? About 35 miles north of The French Quarter in New Orleans, very close to the north shore of Lake Pontchartrain.

From the earliest days, musicians started to cross the lake by steamboat to play for Saturday night dances in the Hall. There were three landing-places for the boats on the shoreline - from east to west the Camellia Landing (destroyed by fire in 1912), the St. Tammany Pier (destroyed by fire in 1926), and the Lewisburg Landing (at the Lewis Plantation). The bands brought plenty of fans with them: Mandeville was considered a fashionable resort. It had several bands playing in various venues, including pavilions, hotels and local park.

Pretty well all the famous early jazz musicians played at The Dew Drop Hall. Buddy Petit, Bunk Johnson, Kid Ory, Tommy Ladnier, Louis Armstrong, Papa Celestin, Sam Morgan, Chester Zardis and George Lewis were among them. Local man Isidore Fritz - according to such witnesses as George Lewis one of the best jazz clarinet players of all time - was a regular there, leading *The Independence Band*, which was hugely popular. He had Tommy Ladnier on trumpet and Edmond Hall on clarinet. Isidore's two brothers also played. What a pity the band was never recorded (or even photographed, it seems). Fritz was unwilling to cross the Lake to play in New Orleans. Why? Because he was doing very nicely in

Mandeville and also had a family building business there. He died in 1940.

Lillian, the wife of banjo-player Buddy Manaday (of Buddy Petit's Band) later recalled that white people as well as black attended and they all got along well together. Petit's Band, by the way, played at many venues in the region - including at Bogalusa, Pensacola and Moss Point.

By the 1920s and 1930s, the Hall was a major centre for jazz concerts. Wooden benches provided limited and basic seating for about 100 people.

But, as fashions and customs changed, the young were no longer interested, the Dew Drop Association ceased to exist and the Hall was virtually abandoned in the mid-1940s. This state of affairs continued for about half a century.

What amazing luck that nobody knocked the building down! All the other similar dance halls of its era were demolished or changed hands and acquired new uses or (like The Sons and Daughters Hall - also in Mandeville, on Lake Shore Drive) burned down.

The overgrown plot was bought at auction in 1993 by Jacqueline 'Jinx' Vidrine. She might have been expected to demolish the building and erect a modern house there; but she was a jazz enthusiast and knew what she was doing. She cleared the plot and investigated the building. She even found an old upright piano inside.

Jacqueline dreamed of re-opening the Hall as a jazz venue or museum. After some years, she managed to get the local Parks Service interested. By 1999, a first concert was possible! Mayor Eddie Price and the Mandeville Council recognised the importance of the property and bought the plot of land from Jacqueline. She herself donated the Hall to the community.

There had been a plan to transport the Hall to a site in Louis Armstrong Park, New Orleans. But the Mayor of Mandeville was easily convinced that the Hall should stay where it was. In 2001 the Hall was placed on the National Register of Historic Places. The 'official' re-opening was on 5 May, 2002. In 2006, two members of the Mandeville City Council led a campaign to create *The Friends of Dew Drop* - a non-profit organisation. There had to be a little refurbishment (at a cost of about 25,000 dollars), but they ensured it was entirely sympathetic with the original design of the Hall.

Concerts featuring the best of local musicians are now put on fortnightly in the Spring and Autumn. There are string bands, jug bands and various similar groups as well as traditional jazz bands.

I'm thrilled to say that 'Jinx' is still very much involved in helping with activities at the Hall. She was there and I had the honour of being introduced to her.

If you go to a Dew Drop concert, you have a choice between standing, or arriving early to secure one of those wooden seats, or (bringing your picnic chairs) listening from outside to the wonderful music drifting through the large open windows (three on each side). Good Louisiana food is usually on sale outside the Hall, as it was in the earliest days.

I hope you will enjoy a short video I made when I visited The Dew Drop:

https://www.youtube.com/watch?v=hW2dYVGZgI4

THE ORIGINS OF TRADITIONAL JAZZ

A most interesting experience when I visited New Orleans in April 2015 was being taken on a conducted tour of the immediate neighbourhood, with John McCusker as guide.

A graduate of Loyola University, New Orleans, John was for thirty years a regional photo-journalist with the Times-Picayune newspaper. He achieved distinction in that work - especially through his coverage of Hurricane Katrina. John is a knowledgeable, lively and well-prepared speaker. He has spent years researching the origins of jazz in New Orleans. The fruits of much of John's research are to be found in his book *Creole Trombone: Kid Ory and the Early Years of Jazz* (University of Mississippi Press, 2012). His findings are convincing because he supports them so well with evidence - such as reports from contemporary newspapers. He is also very proud of being a New Orleans citizen and he loves the early jazz music.

John reminded us of the usual 'myths' and said there may be grains of truth in them, but that essentially they were misleading and should be dispelled. For example, he had found that all these myths were only partially true:

1. Musicians acquired instruments 'left over' by bands after the Civil War and somehow taught themselves to play. (McCusker asks: Why should they do that? There were plenty of new and second-hand musical instruments available cheaply in shops; and there was a strong tradition of young people - black and white - having music lessons in those pre-radio, pre-TV days.)

2. Lots of the early jazz players used to play in the bordellos of Storyville until it was closed down in 1917. (McCusker asks: Why

would you want to waste time with musicians in a bordello? Only a few of the more fancy establishments booked musicians. There were plenty of other places - such as Lakeside - for musicians to find employment.)

3. After the closure of Storyville, the musicians went 'up the river' to Chicago. (McCusker says: Only a tiny proportion of the New Orleans musicians moved north. Most stayed in New Orleans and continued to work there. In any case, if you go 'up river', it doesn't lead to Chicago!)

What Mr. McCusker wanted to impress upon us was that there was a very strong musical tradition in New Orleans. We have to remember there was no TV, no radio and no cinema in those days. At the time, a musical instrument was a 'must have' in most households, just as a computer is today. It was very common to find a mandolin or violin in the home (an interview with the early New Orleans musician Johnny Wiggs confirmed this). And there could well be a concertina, a piano or a harmonium.

Plenty of people made a living teaching youngsters to play musical instruments - piano, string, brass, reeds and so on. Music-making in the home and in public places was commonplace.

John stressed the importance of *opera* in the lives of the citizens. People loved it. There were three well-attended opera houses, so everyone knew the tunes from Verdi, Offenbach, Bizet, Reyer, Von Flotow, Massenet, Meyerbeer and Gounod. What an inspiration to early jazz musicians and composers they must have been!

John McCusker told us the Minstrel Shows and Vaudeville - both well attended in the theatres of New Orleans - were of huge importance (usually underestimated) in the early development of jazz. Likewise the 'society orchestras' (made up of trained sight-reading musicians) influenced the approach of such early New Orleans jazz musicians as Kid Ory.

Of special significance were the crazes for syncopated piano music (ragtime), brass band marches and especially the Blues with its genesis in the depths of African culture. The early jazz musicians also worked at a golden time in popular music, when so many of the hit songs were easy to adapt to a 'jazzy' presentation.

Of course, he told us about Buddy Bolden and took us to some of the places where he used to play. We saw his house and the houses (or sites) where other early jazz stars lived - Nick La Rocca's house, for example. He told us about the early life of Louis Armstrong and he impressed upon us the importance of Edward 'Kid' Ory both as a developer of jazz in the early days and as the man who first recognised the talent of the teenager Louis and set him on his way by booking him for gigs. Ory - who ran his own band in New Orleans from 1907 - also employed such musicians as Johhny Dodds, King Oliver and Sidney Bechet.

John McCusker told us the brass bands became possible only in the mid-Nineteenth Century, after the invention of valved brass instruments (which made all notes of the scales obtainable). In the USA, as in England, there was a massive development of the brass band movement from about 1850 onwards. In England, it eventually became formalised, with national contests, and rules about the numbers of each type of instrument. But in Louisiana matters were more free-style. There were some small and medium-sized bands, undoubtedly forerunners of later jazz bands. In such informal groupings, it would be easy for a player or two to set a fashion for 'jazzing up' a tune.)

From the early days, when the famous benevolent societies operated around New Orleans (they provided mutual help at times of hardship), these social clubs had their own bands; and the bands played at members' funerals.

We tend to think of 'jazz funerals' as a twentieth-century invention. But they are really just a continuation of brass band funerals from long before. John McCusker quoted from a newspaper report of 1857 in which mention was made of the brass band accompanying the coffin.

John took us to various sites including 'Congo Square'. This area had been allocated to the black slaves as a place where on Sundays they were allowed to congregate, play their music and dance. The exciting African dances and the rhythms of their music appealed to all kinds of visitors and onlookers. In these, too, we find a huge influence in the early development of jazz. These Sunday events died out but the Square was used for brass band concerts at the end of the Nineteenth Century.

There is a super video made by John McCusker which enables YOU to go on his conducted tour. May I strongly recommend that you have a look? You can find it on YouTube:

https://www.youtube.com/watch?v=CszEF7d03po

KING OLIVER'S CREOLE JAZZ BAND: THE GENNETT RECORDINGS

Some of the most important recordings in the history of our music were made in 1923. I am referring to the 14 tunes *King Oliver's Creole Jazz Band* recorded in April and October that year for Gennett Records in Richmond, Indiana.

You can enjoy all of the tunes on YouTube and I hope you will have great pleasure discovering them - or exploring them again - for yourselves. You could start here:

https://www.youtube.com/watch?v=kgija2k4Zlc

The Gennett Company had been set up only six years earlier and was still using fairly primitive pre-electric recording methods.

The tunes were:

Alligator Hop

Canal Street Blues

Dippermouth Blues (King Oliver was nick-named 'Dippermouth' because he used to keep on the bandstand a bucket of water with a dipper in it)

Chimes Blues

Just Gone

Snake Rag

Sugarfoot Stomp

Working Man Blues

Zulu's Ball

(all the above were composed or co-written by Oliver himself)

AND

Froggie More

I'm Going Away to Wear You Off My Mind

Krooked Blues

179

Mandy Lee Blues
Weatherbird Rag.

We have only to read that list to appreciate what a contribution Oliver made to the history and repertoire of traditional jazz. (It is often forgotten that he also wrote *Doctor Jazz*. I have sometimes heard band-leaders, announcing this tune, wrongly say that it was composed by Jelly Roll Morton. We must also remember that it was Oliver who later composed those classics *Snag It* and *West End Blues.*)

But these Gennett recordings are also important because they are regarded as the first to document well an authentic black traditional New Orleans jazz band. (In fact, Kid Ory's band had made half a dozen recordings just a few months earlier - for the Nordskog company.)

So who was Oliver?

Cornet player Joe Nathan 'King' Oliver was born on 11 May 1885. Unfortunately, he lost the sight of one eye in his childhood. But by 1908 he was playing in several bands in New Orleans, including the famous marching bands. He worked with Kid Ory and the two of them moved to Chicago in 1918. They joined *Bill Johnson's Original Creole Jazz Band*. Bill Johnson at the time was 47 years old. He played bass and banjo and was an elder statesman and entrepreneur in the music business. He had toured and made New Orleans jazz known outside the South. His band currently played at *The Dreamland Ballroom* in West Van Buren Street, close to the centre of the City of Chicago. (The building has long since disappeared.)

We have to remember that, in those days, the movies and radio were in their infancy; television and computers were things of the future. Most people went out for entertainment. So this was a

180

boom time for dancing, for dance bands and for jazz bands. In Chicago there were plenty of cafés, bars, ballrooms and clubs where you could hear such bands.

As well as *The Dreamland Ballroom*, think of *The Royal Gardens Ballroom*, *The De Luxe Café*, *The Sunset Café*, *Kelly's Stables*, *The Nest* (later *The Apex Club* - of 'Apex Blues' fame), *The Plantation* and *Friar's Inn*. *The Royal Gardens Ballroom* (which regularly accommodated 1000 people) burned down and was replaced by *The Lincoln Gardens*; and that is where Oliver's Creole Jazz Band had its residency.

This was some way south from *The Dreamland Ballroom* - at 459 East 31st Street. As far as I can tell, the Lincoln Gardens Ballroom was bulldozed years ago and - with the help of Mr. Google - I found a glass office block on the site today.

It seems that Bill Johnson was quite happy to hand on his own band to the younger man - King Oliver - to develop in his own way and then to evolve it into *King Oliver's Creole Jazz Band*.

Who played in Oliver's Creole Jazz Band?

Everyone thinks first of Louis Armstrong, because he went on to become a big star in the entertainment world and in the movies. He was to develop a phenomenal technique, a great tone, and virtuoso skill in improvising solo choruses. But in 1923, he was a junior member of Oliver's band - and we should not forget that. However, there's a clear and very enjoyable hint of future glories in the famous solo that Armstrong takes in *Chimes Blues*. Oliver had invited him to move to Chicago from New Orleans and this was the launching pad for Armstrong's stellar career. When you think of the energy and stamina needed for the band's performances (playing for dances long into the night), it is easy to understand why Oliver invited Armstrong to join and help him: it must have been a huge strain on Oliver's lip to sustain such long, hard gigs, with few breaks from playing.

But more important than Armstrong at the time, in my opinion, was the clarinet player Johnny Dodds (1892 - 1940). He had also worked with Kid Ory in New Orleans from 1912. Dodds made a huge contribution to the ensemble style and sound of Oliver's band: his fluency and his soulful, bluesy playing and tone have been an inspiration to generations of clarinet players. In a tune such as *Canal Street Blues*, his decorative runs around the melody and his memorable solo are outstanding. But listen for him even on lesser-known numbers such as *Just Gone* and *Mandy Lee Blues* and you will be impressed. I suppose it was Johnny's good fortune that the clarinet could be heard so clearly, despite the primitive recording process of the time.

Then there was Bill Johnson himself (1872 - 1972), the bass player and former leader who had achieved much even before King Oliver (at Johnson's invitation) became established in Chicago. It is said that he had to switch to banjo in the Gennett studio because the bass would record badly and spoil the sound.

Of enormous importance (and much under-rated by jazz history in my opinion) was the band's pianist Lil Hardin. She had been born in Memphis on 3 Feb 1898 and had worked for some time on the Chicago music scene: she had studied music at Fisk University, obtaining a diploma there, and had played with various bands, including one of her own, even before her partnership with Oliver.

I think hers must have been one of the principal 'brains' shaping the band's music-making. Lil was also the co-composer (with Oliver) of *Alligator Hop*, *Just Gone* and *Working Man Blues*. My guess is that she had a big say in the arrangements of the band's tunes and possibly even in organizing the many two-bar breaks that occur in several of them and which listeners have often thought to be magically spontaneous (such as the famous breaks involving Joe and Louis together in *Snake Rag*). Lil's playing throughout these recordings is a model for all later pianists in New Orleans-style bands - solidly providing the chords on the beat and yet capable of a pretty solo chorus if required, as in *I'm Going Away to Wear You Off My Mind*. And how moving it is to hear those piano chimes of hers coming to us across more than nine decades in *Chimes Blues*!

Within the next three years, after marrying Louis Armstrong, Lil composed (originally for Louis' *Hot Five*) such core tunes in our repertoire as *Knee Drops, I'm Not Rough, Lonesome Blues, Skid-Dat-De-Dat, Two Deuces, Hotter Than That, Jazz Lips, Droppin' Shucks* and *Struttin' With Some Barbecue*. Her other compositions include *Perdido Street Blues, Papa Dip, Tears,* and *Gatemouth*. What an achievement!

Lil died on 27 August 1971.

The trombonist in Oliver's band was Honoré Dutrey (1894 - 1935). He had played in bands in New Orleans. He joined the Navy in 1917 and had an accident that damaged his lungs and eventually caused his premature death. Dutrey strikes me as just right for this band - keeping things simple but always accurate. A good clear illustration of his style is to be heard on *Working Man Blues*.

Warren 'Baby' Dodds, 24-years-old at the time of the recordings, is one of the all-time best drummers. He too had started in New Orleans and had played with Ory there, before working on the riverboats. He was of course the younger brother of Johnny Dodds. In these Gennett recordings, you do not hear the full range of his kit but his presence is strongly felt throughout. Enjoy his breaks on the wood blocks in *Weather Bird Rag*.

Other occasional band members (only on the October Gennett recordings) were Johnny St. Cyr (banjo) and the less-known Paul Anderson 'Stump' Evans (C melody sax).

The recordings were made without the benefit of electricity or microphones. The sound had to be picked up through a large megaphone-funnel. Certain musical instruments had to be omitted or restricted in use because their effect would spoil or unbalance the recording (Baby Dodds could use only part of his drum kit, and Johnson could not use his string bass). The players had to be positioned at various distances from the funnel, to achieve some kind of balance.

Clearly, what we hear on the records is not exactly how the band normally sounded at Lincoln Gardens. But the wonderful polyphony and energy are captured really well.

The tunes are all multi-part, with tricky arrangements, including introductions and codas. There's none of the simple repetition of one 32-bar theme, such as we are offered these days in most performances by traditional jazz bands.

Oliver was proud and professional in his attitude to work and expected the highest standards from his musicians. He was strongly self-disciplined. He drove his band hard. Baby Dodds in an interview years later stated how strenuously all the band members worked at gigs: they would really exhaust themselves. Sure enough, *all* members of the band sound constantly so busy. Listen again to *Dippermouth Blues* and judge for yourself.

Oliver's personal interest in tone (he produced a throaty vocal sound on his cornet) and the use of mutes have had a massive influence on brass players ever since. You can sample his tone and his mutes throughout but of course they are specially conspicuous in *Dippermouth Blues*.

On top of all this, also in 1923, calling his band simply *King Oliver's Jazz Band* (drawn from a pool of players that included Barney Bigard, Paul Barbarin, Kid Ory, Luis Russell and others as well as those of the *Creole Jazz Band*), Oliver also recorded in Chicago for the Okeh, Paramount and Columbia labels a total of 23 numbers, such as *Riverside Blues, Mabel's Dream, Southern Stomps, Tears, Buddy's Habit, Sweet Lovin' Man, High Society, Sobbin' Blues*, and *Camp Meeting Blues* - and others.

But Oliver's Creole Jazz Band of 1923 was short-lived. It disintegrated the following year. Oliver went on to play in various combinations and bands (sometimes run by himself). His struggles and decline have been well documented. And it is sad to think he died in poverty on 10 April 1938.

Listening to all these Gennett recordings again has made me realise what an example to us all King Oliver's band of 1923 was. That's the way to do it. Many others have set out to emulate his music. But there's nothing quite like the originals.

LOUIS DUMAINE, ARMAND PIRON AND SAM MORGAN

If you want to know what the authentic New Orleans bands sounded like in the 1920s, it's easy to study some fine examples. We must be grateful to the original sound recordists and to all who have perpetuated their work by means of various technologies over the decades and - more recently - those who have put the music on to YouTube.

I'm thinking at the moment of three bands in particular. Their total recorded output is not huge; but there is plenty from which we can learn, with careful study.

Louis Dumaine's Jazzola Eight recorded only four tunes. The pieces themselves don't get much attention these days, but the recordings are a lesson to all traditional jazz musicians in how their instrument should contribute to an effective ensemble. These repay close scrutiny. For an example:

https://www.youtube.com/watch?v=odY4zbfBRc4

Next, think of Armand Piron (violinist) and his classy orchestra. They gave us lovely performances of such numbers as these (mostly composed by the band members):

Bouncing Around
I Wish I Could Shimmy Like My Sister Kate
Mamma's Gone, Goodbye
Kiss Me Sweet
Bright Star Blues
Louisiana Swing
Red Man Blues
Sud Bustin' Blues

For an example of a typical well-arranged piece (with great ensemble work) that many of us still try to emulate:

https://www.youtube.com/watch?v=K7HuZNF77IQ

Then there's the eight-piece Sam Morgan's Band (with big Jim Robinson on trombone). It recorded just eight tunes in 1927. They included *Bogalusa Strut*, *Mobile Stomp* and *Short Dress Girl* (all composed by Morgan) as well as three spirituals, notably *Over in the Gloryland*, which is still very popular. These recordings powerfully influenced the repertoire and drive of many of today's bands. For a stomping performance that gives you the full flavour of this band:

https://www.youtube.com/watch?v=fIIQutjtjtc

LUTHJENS: A LITTLE PIECE OF JAZZ HISTORY

I have long been vaguely aware that there once was a 'Luthjens Dance Hall' somewhere in New Orleans and that our mid-Twentieth Century traditional jazz heroes played there. But it was not until The Shotgun Jazz Band announced that they had recorded their 2014 CD entitled 'Yearning' at Luthjens that my curiosity was further aroused. (The CD, by the way, presents the music with a wonderfully clear 'empty hall' acoustic.)

I have set out to discover what I can about Luthjens and I learned, for example, that there had been an earlier Luthjens Dance Hall at a different location.

Here's the story. There has always been a great fondness for dancing in New Orleans, so it is not surprising that many dance halls sprang up. Obviously they gave plentiful employment to musicians. Having a good night out was not too expensive. The halls themselves would be sparsely furnished. There were bare wooden tables and simple chairs or benches. Luthjens Dance Hall was situated in the 1200 block of Franklin Avenue (I think at the junction with Marais Street).

The location, among quiet tree-lined streets, was pleasant. It was about a mile north-east of the French Quarter.

How did the Hall get its name? It was established by Mrs. Clementine Luthjens, who was born in New Orleans in 1880. Probably there was some German ancestry - at least on her husband's side: there had been plenty of migration of German people with the surname 'Luthjens' (or, more commonly 'Lutjens' without the 'h', I guess becoming 'Luthjens' in the USA).

She bought the humble, unpretentious building (previously a seafood restaurant) and set it up as a 'beer parlor and dance hall'. Steadfastly, she employed only the authentic old-style black jazzmen. She wanted the establishment to be family-friendly: she liked couples to bring the children. (However, it later acquired the nickname 'The Old Folks' Home': its patrons tended to be elderly white people.)

Informal dress was encouraged. Prices charged for drinks were reasonable. So it was the most economical venue in New Orleans if you wanted to hear the *good 'ol'-fashioned* jazz; and tourists sought it out. Dancing took place on Fridays, Saturdays and Sundays. On the other nights of the week, Luthjens was merely a kind of bistro, complete with a juke-box.

Many of the legendary musicians of the mid-Twentieth Century played there. Emile Barnes is believed to have led the first band. Later came such players as Big Eye Louis Nelson, George Lewis, Joseph Bourgeau, Alton Purnell, 'Slow Drag' Pavageau, Lawrence Marrero, Harrison Brazlee, Louis Gallaud, George Henderson, Alcide Landry, Ernest Rogers, Benny Turner, Peter Bocage, and Charlie Love; and in the final years the virtual 'house band' was that of De De and Billie Pierce.

The patrons liked the more stately forms of dancing and disapproved of 'jitterbugging'! The two-step, the one-step and the waltz were mostly in demand.

It was quite a small building. So I imagine that - if you had a band and about 60 dancers in there - it would have felt crowded. The band was 'protected' from collisions with dancers by being placed at one end of the hall on a small bandstand two feet off the floor, (as at The Dew Drop Hall).

189

Sadly, the Luthjens Dance Hall burnt down in the early hours of Saturday, 30 January, 1960, with the loss of the lives of both Mrs. Clementine Luthjens (then aged 81) and her son Jules (aged 50), who were living in the back apartment of the premises. By that time, Mrs. Luthjens was a wheelchair-bound invalid. I wonder whether her son died while trying to save her: we shall never know. Perhaps it is not surprising that a fire - even in a one-storey building - could have had such dreadful consequences: it seems to have been a flimsy wooden structure, covered by tar-paper. Perhaps a smouldering cigarette end, left by a customer, caused the fire. Apparently smoking 'while dancing' was forbidden, but I suppose there was plenty of smoking by customers relaxing at tables.

Clementine's nephew Jerome Luthjens in 1961 opened a new Luthjens at 2300 Chartres (at the corner of Chartres and Marigny Streets - less than a mile from the original building). This was a more substantial brick-built hall, again of one storey, though with a flat roof. It was about half a mile nearer to the Mississippi, or - to put it another way - a mere 250 metres east of the present-day Frenchmen Street jazz bars, such as The Spotted Cat, The Three Muses, and The Maison. It too was in a pleasant, leafy area, among pretty houses - many of them of the 'Shotgun' type.

Jerome Luthjens ran this dance hall until his death in 1975. It continued in business under the management of his widow Louise until 1981, when it finally closed.

In more recent times, the area has been re-classified as a 'residential zone' and Luthjens no longer has a liquor licence. About one-third of the building is now occupied by a recording studio.

This was where, in 2014, The Shotgun Jazz Band made their CD. They chose not to use the main studio's facilities or equipment. They just set up on the stage as if at a regular gig and used a combination of room microphones and and close microphones.

The resulting product was excellent and nostalgic. Amy Johnson filmed them in the Hall while they were recording one of the tunes. You can watch her video:

https://www.youtube.com/watch?v=5Rh52iL41gI

Although there is no audience present, it gives us an idea of what it was like to play there, especially as this band has so much in common with the De De Pierce Band of half a century earlier.

By the way, the name is sometimes given as *Luthjen's Dance Hall*; but this is the result of a punctuation error. Mrs. Luthjens' name definitely ended with the 's'. It should be written *Luthjens' Dance Hall* or *Luthjens Dance Hall*.

THOSE LADIES OF THE BLUES

Tell me honestly: were you much aware of Lucille Bogan, Mamie Smith, Merline Johnson, Memphis Minnie, Clara Smith and Hattie Hart before Tuba Skinny and other young bands in New Orleans today revived some of their songs? I certainly wasn't. Yes, I knew about Bessie Smith and Ma Rainey, and I was aware of Victoria Spivey and Clara Smith, though I couldn't have told you much about them.

So I must thank Tuba Skinny and others for making me seek out those great lady performers (who were often composers too) from the 1920s and 1930s. Fortunately, quite of a lot of their work is available on YouTube.

Lucille Bogan (in her later years performing as Bessie Jackson) lived from 1897 until 1948, first in Mississippi and later in Alabama. She was twice married. Lucille made a lot of recordings, songs often composed by herself; and some of them are notable for their sexual innuendoes or even explicitness. She was the originator of *Tricks Ain't Walking No More*. Memphis Minnie recorded it too. This Century, it has become a favourite in Tuba Skinny's repertoire. Lucille's recording probably also influenced their choice of Eddie Miller's composition *I'd Rather Drink Muddy Water*.

Merline Johnson was probably born in 1912, in Mississippi or Missouri. She made recordings from 1937 until 1947, usually in the company of some of the most famous blues musicians of that era. If you are a fan, you may be interested to know that it was from Merline Johnson that Tuba Skinny learned *Got a Man in the 'Bama Mine, Sold It To The Devil*, and *Running Down My Man*. What a legacy from someone about whom little is known!

Hattie Hart worked both with and apart from The Memphis Jug Band. Among the songs she recorded that Tuba Skinny have taken up were *Won't You Be Kind To Me?* (her 1928 composition), *Ambulance Man,* and *Papa's Got Your Bath Water On.*

Not much is known about Hattie, who was born in Memphis, Tennessee, in about 1900.

I must briefly mention Clara Smith, who was born around 1894 in Carolina and worked in both New Orleans and New York. In the 1920s, she recorded well over a hundred songs, often with some of the 'big names'. Though she did not compose it, Clara made *Freight Train Blues* famous; and this is another song Tuba Skinny have developed dramatically (train noises and all) in their repertoire.

Among Clara's other interesting recordings are *Jelly Bean Blues* and *Percolatin' Blues.* Clara died in 1935.

And what about Mamie Smith (1883 - 1946 - no relation to the other Smiths)? She was the singer who made famous the song composed in 1920 by the 27-year-old Perry Bradford, *Crazy Blues.* He was the Musical Director of *Mamie Smith and Her Jazz Hounds.* Mamie recorded it in the same year with huge success. This is now considered by jazz and blues scholars to have been an important milestone in the history of our music, because Mamie was the first black blues singer to be recorded.

Mamie could be said to have started the era of classic female blues. In 2014, Tuba Skinny introduced into their repertoire a super version of *Crazy Blues* - quite a tour de force by their singer Erika Lewis.

Memphis Minnie has become a favourite of mine. It was she who recorded *Me and My Chauffeur, Bumblebee, Blood Thirsty*

193

Blues, Frisco Town, I'm Goin' Back Home, What's The Matter With The Mill? as well as many other good old songs. Erika Lewis and Tuba Skinny have found her work to be a rich source.

'Memphis Minnie' was of course a stage name. She was born in Algiers (the 'across the river' suburb of New Orleans) in 1897 and her real name was Lizzie Douglas. As a teenager, she became a busker in Memphis and it was there that her musical career was to take off, especially when she was invited to make recordings, together with her second husband (of three): they were billed as 'Kansas Joe and Memphis Minnie'. They wrote a lot of their own material. Over the years, Minnie performed in many different cities and recorded for various labels. She had a hard life but seems to have been a tough, resilient, cheerful woman and a good singer and guitarist. Possibly she was the most popular country blues singer of all time. She died in 1973. Fortunately, it is still possible to buy many of her recordings and to find some on YouTube. For a very pleasant and well recorded example of her work:

https://www.youtube.com/watch?v=rD2GUKwqliU

As for Victoria Spivey from Houston, this lady had a long career. Coming from a musical family, she lived from 1906 until 1976 and was a prolific entertainer.

She was a pianist as well as a singer and composer. (Among her compositions were *TB Blues, How Do They Do It That Way?, Black Snake Blues, Detroit Moan, Moaning the Blues, Long Gone,* and *Spider Web Blues*.) She made her first recording in 1926 and her last as late as 1964, having worked at times with several of the big names of jazz. At the age of 56, she launched a record label of her own. She even found time to marry four husbands. To appreciate Victoria Spivey singing *Any Kind A Man Would Be Better Than You,* listen to this:

https://www.youtube.com/watch?v=XZ06tV2QnVQ

You will understand at once how much she has influenced today's singers, such as Erika Lewis.

Georgia White was another blues singer who influenced them. For example, Erika Lewis picked up *Late Hour Blues* from Georgia's 1939 recording of this song by Richard M. Jones. Georgia and Richard worked together and jointly composed *I'm Blue and Lonesome; Nobody Cares For Me* and *Biscuit Roller* - both of them songs Erika has adopted - to the delight of her fans. Georgia White is believed to have been born in 1903 and was working in Chicago by the 1920s.

She made a very large number of recordings. She was still performing as late as the 1960s and is believed to have died in about 1980.

HOW THOSE OLD TUNES WERE PASSED DOWN

The names, content and shapes of some of the good old jazz tunes have become confused over the past century. Studying the old classics can be hard work.

Here's the kind of thing that happened over the decades. (I'm using an imaginary tune that I will call *Moss Point Rag*.)

First, in 1908, a minor composer in Missouri (classically-trained and influenced by the structures of classical music), produces a tune he calls *Moss Point Rag*. It is published as piano sheet music, running to 6 sides of paper. *Moss Point Rag* comprises three sections in G, followed by a change of key to C for the fourth theme - the 'Trio'. It is an attractive, merry piece of music, full of subtleties, syncopations, elaborate decorations of the melody and complexities.

Between 1910 and the Second World War, music of this kind (of which there is plenty preserved in the university archives of America) gives the pianists in the bar-rooms of New Orleans and Chicago the chance to show off their considerable skills.

At the same time, the early dance-bands and jazz-bands (with anything from three to ten musicians) are attracted by *Moss Point Rag* and want to play it. But they cannot possibly play it as written: the complexities you see in the music above are fair enough for a pianist's fingers, but the melody-playing trumpet or cornet at the heart of the band could not be expected to cope with them. Even a virtuoso player would soon be exhausted if he had to produce such a flow of notes (including many high ones) for a whole evening's gig.

So the bands play *Moss Point Rag* in their own way. They simplify the melodies, sometimes using a cornet (or violin in the earliest days) with clarinet to do what they can to share the tricky bits. They capture the essence of the melody, rather than its many decorative notes. Some of them leave out the section called the 'Trio', because they find it less interesting or too difficult. They add a new section, either of their own invention or plagiarised from a different composition.

For an example of this sort of thing happening, consider *Hilarity Rag*, composed by James Scott in 1910. To see the sheet music and hear how it sounded as a piano piece:

https://www.youtube.com/watch?v=Sx-0R_Zotxw

But to hear how it was re-interpreted and simplified when a jazz band got hold of it:

https://www.youtube.com/watch?v=obMZmrku25w

You see what I mean?

So to get back to my story, in 1928, a band based in Chicago uses just the first two themes (much simplified) from *Moss Point Rag*, puts them into the key of Bb for convenience and records a version under a new name, *Uptown Strut.*

Towards the end of this period, a clever bandleader-arranger in New York records with his band a new tune called *Spring Street Stomp* but later researchers will find it is suspiciously similar to *Moss Point Rag*!

After the War, during the Bebop era, the tune is rarely heard in any form.

But twenty years later, in what has been called the New Orleans (or Dixieland) Revival, young traditional jazz bands again blossom in the USA, in Europe and in the rest of the world. A bandleader in England picks up the old 78rpm Chicago recording of *Uptown Strut* from 1928, works out his own version of it by ear and gets his band to record it. Many pub bands buy the record, like it and introduce it into their repertoire.

In their turn, these Revivalists inevitably and unwittingly make further slight changes. Maybe they have to guess at some of the notes that are indistinct on the scratchy old records.

So the band (I'm now talking 1950 – 1965) plays its own version: each player has it in his head but the chances are that it is never written down.

The late Ray Foxley (he died in 2002) was the pianist in Ken Colyer's band. Ray once told me he would learn tunes from those old 78 rpm records a few bars at a time – first listening and then working out the notes and chords on his piano.

Move on another 30 years and you find traditional jazz in decline again, though still with enough bands and enthusiasts throughout the world to keep it going as a minority art form. *Uptown Strut* is in their repertoire, with the composer usually credited as 'Anon' or 'Trad'.

Here are some of the old tunes still passed on from band to band in one form or another:

Blame it on the Blues (also known as *Quincy Street Stomp*), *At a Georgia Camp Meeting*, *Big Chief Battleaxe*, *Bluebells Goodbye* (also known as *Bright Eyes Goodbye*), *Bugle Boy March* (also known as *The American Soldier*), *Ce Mossieu Qui Parle* (maybe originally *C'est Moi Seul Qui Parle*), *Chrysanthemum Rag*, *Climax Rag* (also known as *Astoria Strut*), *Creole Belles*, *Dill Pickles*, *Don't Go 'way, Nobody* (almost identical to several other tunes, such as *Everybody's Talking About Sammy*), *Dusty Rag* and *Thriller Rag* (both composed by a lady from Indianapolis), *Golden Leaf Strut* (also known as *Milenberg Joys* -

main theme), *Grace and Beauty, Gettysburg March, Hiawatha Rag, Jenny's Ball, Kinklets, Maple Leaf Rag, Moose March, Shim-Me-Sha-Wobble, 1919 March* (also known as *The Rifle Rangers*), *Ostrich Walk, Panama Rag, Salutation March* (probably a Victorian quadrille originally), *Silver Bell* (also known as *Sometimes My Burden* - second theme), *Smoky Mokes, Snake Rag, That Teasing Rag*, and *Uptown Bumps*. And how on earth did *Ta-Wa-Bac-A-Wa* become *The Bucket's Got a Hole In It?*

I doubt whether you could walk into a music shop today and buy the authentic printed original music for any of these.

THE MEMPHIS JUG BAND

The links between the early 'jug bands' and traditional jazz are much stronger than you may think. Their repertoires and playing styles overlapped, as did their instrumentation. Also the jug bands tended to play tunes based on simple, familiar chord sequences - just the sort of thing that appeals to many traditional jazz musicians.

And don't be put off by the thought of 'jugs'. You may be picturing someone trying to make 'music' by blowing into a jug and producing a sound like a constipated tuba. But in fact jug bands comprised various mixtures of fine musicians playing guitars, banjos, mandolins, violins, pianos - in fact all manner of instruments (and yes, often including a jug). There could be anything from two to eight players in the band. These bands flourished in the late 1920s and early 1930s, especially in the regions of Memphis and Chicago.

In recent years, they have had a big influence on the young generation of busking traditional jazz players and string bands in the streets of New Orleans; and there are also numerous modern jug bands playing material taken from the 1920s.

Think for example of the following tunes in the repertoire of many young bands today. They were all learned from the records made by *The Memphis Jug Band*:

I'll See You In The Spring
Papa's Got Your Bathwater On
Fourth Street Mess Around
Bumble Bee
Ambulance Man

Care to try one? Listen to a performance of *I'll See You in the Spring*:

https://www.youtube.com/watch?v=sSL-sioygqc

Compare it with The Memphis Jug Band's original:

https://www.youtube.com/watch?v=h2Sp78E8WPQ

But who exactly were *The Memphis Jug Band*? Like many of today's young street bands, they did not have a fixed personnel. The driving force was Will Shade (also known as Son Brimmer or Sun Brimmer): he was a singer who played guitar and harmonica. He composed several of the band's songs. From 1926, he convened the band and managed such gigs as they attracted. He drew on a pool of fourteen musicians who could play banjo, guitar, mandolin, washboard, kazoo, violin, jug, drums and piano. They included Vol Stevens, Charlie Nickerson and Ben Ramey. Four lady singers (notably Hattie Hart and Memphis Minnie) also appeared at various times on the recordings. They played blues, ballads, novelty humorous numbers and pop songs of the day. They produced a distinctive, addictive sound, partly because the jug and kazoo respectively performed the roles of trombone and trumpet in a traditional jazz band. They are believed to have made almost 100 recordings (more of which you can find on YouTube). The band also occasionally recorded under different names (such as *The Memphis Sheiks*, *The Carolina Peanut Boys* and *The Dallas Jug Band*).

Overlapping other local jug bands at this time were *The South Memphis Jug Band*, *Gus Cannon's Jug Stompers* and *Jed Davenport's Beale Street Jug Band*.

The Memphis Jug Band went on, widening its styles and membership, over many years; but it is the early recordings that

201

have most influenced traditional jazz today. Of course, the band's legacy to pop and rock music has been even greater.

Among its repertoire, let me recommend these (all of which I believe you can find on YouTube). Note that many of its tunes were 12-bar blues.

On The Road Again

Stealin' Stealin' (a 32-bar a - a - b - a)

Round and Round (great fun)

Kansas City Blues

Move That Thing (rather like *It's Tight Like That*)

He's in the Jailhouse Now (series of verses about criminals who have been punished, each followed by the 'He's in the Jailhouse Now' 16-bar chorus)

K.C. Moan (a very simple blues, but in 16 bars)

Papa's Got Your Bathwater On (sung as a duet, and with lyrics alleged to refer to an ancient voodoo practice)

Gator Wobble (standard 12-bar)

I'll See You In The Spring (mentioned above - a lovely 8+8 bar sung structure, using the Magnolia Chord Sequence, with a curious 14-bar instrumental intermezzo [faithfully retained in the Tuba Skinny version] between the vocals)

She Done Sold It Out (standard 12-bar)

Fourth Street Mess Around (great sung number, 16+16 bar structure; with an amusing Coda)

Bumble Bee (archetypical 12-bar country blues. Singing by Memphis Minnie makes it something special)

Ambulance Man (another 12-bar duet)

I'm Looking For The Bully of the Town (Despite its off-putting title, this up-tempo song from 1927 is surprisingly catchy.)

THE GRINNELL GIGGERS

The Grinnell Giggers were a small string band - usually just three players - who performed near the Missouri-Arkansas border in the 1920s and 1930s. They were based about 700 miles south-east of the centre of the USA. Or, to put it another way, 500 miles due north of New Orleans.

These men were farmers and fishermen, whose hobby was providing music for country dances. Their leader was Ben Tinnon, born in 1890. He played the violin and also composed most of their tunes. His pieces were bright and simple, with two or three good melodic themes based on familiar easy chord sequences - just right for dancing and straightforward and playing. Try, for example, *Ruth's Rag*, which he wrote in honour of his wife, Ruth:

https://www.youtube.com/watch?v=3FomQkfSxQk

Let's get this clear right now: the fact that they called themselves 'Giggers' had nothing to do with playing gigs, in the music sense. Grinnells were fish and 'gigging' was a way of catching them (using a pronged fork). These men really were grinnell giggers.

The only times the band recorded were in May and November 1930. Together with Tinnon on fiddle were Melvin Paul (1905-1970) on banjo or mandolin, and Grover Grant (1897-1971) on guitar. In fact they recorded only eight tunes. But these sessions, which took place in Memphis, have proved to be important and influential.

The tunes recorded were:

Cotton Pickers Drag (*composed by Tinnon himself and probably the best of them all - with a distinctive and memorable second theme, descending from high notes*)

Duck Shoes Rag

Gigger's Waltz 1

Gigger's Waltz 2 (*clearly the same piece of music as above but there are quite a few differences of detail in the playing*)

Plow Boy Hop (*a fine piece by Tinnon*)

Ruth's Rag

Sunset Waltz (*Composed by Tinnon. Yes, a waltz; but it's a different from tune from the 'Sunset Waltz' created and recorded by The Mississippi Mud Steppers the previous year*)

Uncle Ned's Waltz (*a gentle waltz by Tinnon. It has a 'Victorian' feel to it, and there is some pleasant tremolo playing by the banjo*)

A generous uploader codenamed *Banjerholler* has put all these on YouTube for our enjoyment.

As there are a number of fiddle-players among the present young generation of traditional jazz musicians in New Orleans, it is not surprising that that they have been attracted by this music. For example, there is the charming video in which Shaye Cohn is seen playing *Plow Boy Hop* on the fiddle (apparently for her own amusement), and other members of Tuba Skinny gradually join in:

https://www.youtube.com/watch?v=EZtUH6sRD_c

And you may care to watch a video I made in April 2016 of The Rhythm Wizards playing Tinnon's *Cotton Pickers Drag*:

https://www.youtube.com/watch?v=B6LYrMH7b-c

Of the three Grinnell Giggers, Ben Tinnon was the first born and the last to die. He passed away in 1974.

'LOVE SONGS OF THE NILE'

Love Songs of the Nile is a beautiful tune that I first came across when I heard that very fine English trumpeter Cuff Billett playing it with his band in the 1990s. I have since discovered that it has been recorded by many of the best bands.

You can hear it played by De De and Billie Pierce (with George Lewis on clarinet and Louis Nelson on trombone):

https://www.youtube.com/watch?v=AwHmmKuVfuk

The great *Shotgun Jazz Band* of New Orleans has the song in its repertoire. Here's their version:

https://www.youtube.com/watch?v=XK8WX_EzK9Q

This song was written for a 1933 film called 'The Barbarian'; and it was sung in the film by Ramon Navarro. The composers were Nacio Herb Brown and Arthur Freed. (Nacio Herb Brown also wrote *You Stepped out of a Dream* and *You Were Meant for Me*.)

205

'THE CAT'S GOT KITTENS'

One of my friends says every jazz programme should include at least one bit of nonsense. And I know a couple of fans who constantly request *The Cat's Got Kittens* (often written as *The Kat's Got Kittens*).

It is not a tune that's easy to find on YouTube - or anywhere else. I don't know its origin. But the earliest recording of it seems to have been made in New Orleans on 15 May 1945, when the singer was Edward 'Noon' Johnson (1903-1969) and the supporting band included George Lewis, Lawrence Marrero, Baby Dodds, Bunk Johnson and Alcide Pavageau.

The Cat's Got Kittens could have been 'composed' by anybody (maybe Noon himself). All that was needed was to put some nonsense words and a slightly different melodic emphasis to *You Can't Escape From Me (*aka *San Jacinto Stomp*), (words by Charles French, music by Erskine Hawkins and Sammy Lowe). It was published and recorded in 1939.

Fifty years after the Edward 'Noon' Johnson recording, *The Cat's Got Kittens* was popularized by Cliff 'Kid' Bastien (1937-2003), when he played for years in Toronto.

You can access his storming version here - and even purchase it, if you wish. To start the performance, you need to click on the arrow that will appear:

https://patricktevlin.bandcamp.com/track/kats-got-kittens

For a pleasant and clear performance by a British group (*The Black Cat Jazz Band*):

https://www.youtube.com/watch?v=CuZuJ-u92AI

MA RAINEY'S 'DREAM BLUES'

It was in 2013 that I was introduced to Ma Rainey's lovely tune *Dream Blues*. Ma Rainey recorded it (accompanied by the Pruitt Twins) in Chicago in 1924. I believe Ma Rainey herself wrote it that year. You can hear the song on YouTube:

https://www.youtube.com/watch?v=p5JVIh9npu0

It is a conventional 12-bar blues, except for the way it uses the mediant where we might expect the tonic. Note, for example, how the melody ends on G, and not on Eb, as we might expect.

Ma Rainey - sometimes known as *The Mother of the Blues* - was one of the first great blues recording artists. She came from Georgia in the USA and she died in 1959.

'I CAN'T ESCAPE' - 'YOU CAN'T ESCAPE' ?

Here's something we need to sort out.

In 1936, Leo Robin and Richard Whiting composed a song called *I Can't Escape From You*. You can watch Bing Crosby singing it in the 1936 movie 'Rhythm on the Range':

https://www.youtube.com/watch?v=S90cwHsu9k0

Then in 1939, a song called *You Can't Escape From Me* was composed by Charles French (words) and Sammy Lowe and Erskine Hawkins (music). You can hear the Erskine Hawkins Orchestra recording:

https://www.youtube.com/watch?v=FUni_cFxZfM

And in 1944 George Lewis recorded (in the San Jacinto Hall) a tune he called *San Jacinto Stomp*, though it is clearly the Erskine Hawkins tune *You Can't Escape From Me*. Many traditional jazz bands since then have played it under the title *San Jacinto Stomp*.

But, adding to the confusion, *I Can't Escape From You* and *You Can't Escape From Me* are very similar in structure. They use virtually the same chord progression. So it's not surprising that band-leaders often (incorrectly) tell you that *I Can't Escape* is also known as *San Jacinto Stomp*.

The words of *You Can't Escape From Me* are nothing special. On the other hand, the words of *I Can't Escape From You* (you heard them in the Bing Crosby film clip) are fun to sing.

So, it's possible today to play a song you call *I Can't Escape*, actually using the tune of *You Can't Escape*, even though your words are those of *I Can't Escape*! And this is exactly what happens at some performances. Confusing, isn't it?

'CROW JANE' AND 'JACKSON STOMP'

The extraordinary thing about *Jackson Stomp* is that it is 11 bars (measures) in length. Virtually all traditional jazz tunes (in common with most popular music of the first half of the Twentieth Century) are in multiples of FOUR bars. Musicians feel, think and play the music in four-bar phrases. So eleven should not work!

Jackson Stomp is really a 12-bar blues with the ninth bar missing. In theory, it should sound awkward. Yet *Tuba Skinny* always sail through it, chorus after chorus, with their usual brilliant collective improvisations, as if an eleven-bar song was the most natural thing in the world.

And what about *Crow Jane*? I had never heard of this song before Tuba Skinny introduced me to it. Apparently it was made up and recorded by Nehemiah 'Skip' James about 90 years ago!

The tricky thing about this number is that, although it is basically a repetitive eight-bar tune, it also has an optional 2-bar tag.

Tuba Skinny deal with this tag in different ways in their various performances. On their CD version, they choose to have the band playing four choruses of eight bars, then Erika singing five choruses in 10-bar form - apart from the penultimate, which she takes as 8 bars. The band then plays more eight-bar choruses, Erika returns with some ten-bars, and the band rounds things off with choruses of eight bars; and yet there is one more twist: a TWELVE-bar chorus (including a four-bar tag) to finish. Sounds complicated? Yes. But such is the discipline and understanding within this band that nobody trips up, nobody puts a foot wrong. They play it as one. And, as usual, the improvisations on the basic theme are mind-boggling.

Here's a video of Tuba Skinny giving a vigorous street performance of *Jackson Stomp*:

https://www.youtube.com/watch?v=rGuLZfMqIoc

And here they perform *Crow Jane* at a French Quarter Festival:

https://www.youtube.com/watch?v=QFheef624jc

'IN THE SWEET BY AND BY' - AND PIE IN THE SKY

I have often heard people use the expression 'It's all pie in the sky'. I occasionally use it myself. When I say something is 'pie in the sky', I mean it is something that sounds wonderful – as an aspiration – but that it will never actually happen. We shall have to go on putting up with something worse.

But I never knew where this expression originated – until recently.

There is a Victorian song (a hymn or spiritual) called *In the Sweet By-and-By*. It has words by S. Fillmore Bennett and music by Joseph Webster. The tune is simple and very pleasant. It is still often played by traditional jazz bands. The words of the Chorus are:

In the sweet by-and-by
We shall meet on that beautiful shore.
In the sweet by-and-by
We shall meet on that beautiful shore.

A verse states that *our spirits shall sorrow no more.*

Its message is that, however hard things may seem while we're here on Earth, better times will come in Heaven.

But a few years after it was composed, in 1911, there came a man called Joe Hill, who chose to write an alternative set of words for the song. (Joe Hill had been born in Sweden as Joel Haaglund and was an immigrant to the USA in 1902.)

Joe Hill noticed how downtrodden working people were supposed to find consolation in such hymns. He did not like the way religion was being used to keep the labouring, uneducated classes in their place, enduring suffering and hunger, while their masters and bosses led luxurious, comfortable lives. So he wrote some new hard-hitting words on behalf of those downtrodden souls:

Long-haired preachers come out every night,

Try to tell you what's wrong and what's right;

But when asked how 'bout something to eat

They will answer in voices so sweet:

You will eat, bye and bye,

In that glorious land above the sky;

Work and pray, live on hay,

You'll get pie in the sky when you die.

There are several more verses in the same vein – in particular suggesting the bosses should try their hand at hard work:

When you've learned how to cook and how to fry;

Chop some wood, 'twill do you good

Then you'll eat in the sweet bye and bye.

This is powerful satire, with a message about a function of religion that is still relevant today, especially in other parts of the world from those for which it was originally written.

I am specially impressed by the 'pie in the sky'. It is the perfect image to make the point. It so simple and so crisp. The internal rhyme makes it stick in our mind. It is no surprise that it was adopted into everyday currency and is now used in hundreds of contexts Joe Hill could never have imagined. [And a similar expression to *pie in the sky* is of course *jam tomorrow*, which dates from Victorian times. It was used by the White Queen in Lewis Carroll's *Through the Looking Glass*.]

So let's eat a pie and drink a toast to Joe Hill, who incidentally in 1915 was executed by the Utah authorities after being charged for a murder that he almost certainly did not commit. 30,000 angry supporters of Joe attended his funeral. But that's another story.

Incidentally, a similar satirical twist occurred in the calypso-jazz song *Buy Me a Zeppelin*. It's about the joys of touring the globe and discovering new places, like the great explorers of the past - many of whom are mentioned in the lyrics. But in some performances the word 'explorer' is replaced by 'exploiter' and the song becomes a commentary on the evils of colonialism.

'DEEP HENDERSON'

Tuba Skinny added to their repertoire a piece written in 1926 by Fred Rose and first made famous that year by the King Oliver Band. It is called *Deep Henderson.*

They must have worked hard getting this tune into their heads. It is a tricky, complicated piece, including a key change. It has several sections and many moments where the clarinet or the cornet have one-bar breaks or where a beat or two are completely silent. Shaye Cohn once described it as a 'monster piece'! It is also very rhythmic and the overall effect is terrifically exciting.

There are now several videos on YouTube of Tuba Skinny playing this tune. May I recommend that you seek them out?

'DELTA BOUND'

Delta Bound is a great haunting song: it descends through semitones, with a fair sprinkling of minor and diminished chords. It is a 32-bar tune, with the familiar a - a - b - a structure.

Those of us who are fans of *Tuba Skinny* (i.e. almost the entire population of the world) have been introduced to it through the singing of Erika Lewis. It was on *Tuba Skinny*'s CD entitled *Rag Band* - released in 2012.

However, it seems the song dates from as long ago as 1934. It was composed by Alex Hill, who was a jazz pianist in Chicago during the 1920s. Although he worked with many of the 'big names', it is not surprising if you have never heard of Alex Hill. The poor chap lived only to the age of 30.

On YouTube there is a video of Erika singing this song with Tuba Skinny in its early days. View it here:

https://www.youtube.com/watch?v=5u0uqoqfMEM

Erika sings *Delta Bound* in the key of Bb. However (typical of *Tuba Skinny*) the band usually plays a first chorus in the key of F before Erika takes over. The Band also reverts to F to round off the performance.

THE 'ST. LOUIS TICKLE' AND 'BUDDY BOLDEN'S BLUES' MYSTERY

The famous *Buddy Bolden's Blues* is played occasionally by most traditional jazz bands. It's the one beginning with the words 'I thought I heard Buddy Bolden say *You're nasty, you're dirty, take it away....*'.

I'm not the first person to notice that the tune of *Buddy Bolden's Blues* is in fact the second theme in the composition *St. Louis Tickle*.

St. Louis Tickle was composed in about 1904 (when Buddy Bolden was a star on the New Orleans music scene).

The composers were named on the original sheet music as 'Barney and Seymore' (elsewhere 'Seymour'). But it is probable that these names were a pseudonym for Theron Catlan Bennett (1879 - 1937) - who became a well-known composer, music publisher (in Chicago) and music-shop owner (in Denver).

Having examined the sheet music, which is a well-structured through-composed early rag, I assumed that Bolden's Band 'lifted' the second theme from this composition, put words to it and made it their own.

However, internet sources claim the tune was composed by Bolden himself. Or that it was composed by the trombone player in his band - Willie Cornish - or at least that Cornish put the words to it. If Bolden's Band composed it, the composer of *St. Louis Tickle* must have lifted it from them.

But he did not live in New Orleans, so would he even have heard it in those days before mass media? And why would a composer of his obvious talent need to steal an idea for a theme? And how do we account for his distinctively 'raggy' rhythms and notes in Bars 7 and 8 and Bars 14, 15, and 16? They are more subtle and complex than the simplified version used in the song.

My theory would have been that Bolden's band lifted and adapted the tune from *St. Louis Tickle*. But we are confidently assured by the experts that Bennett stole the tune from Bolden and sneaked the melody into his composition.

Whatever the truth, *Buddy Bolden's Blues* exists and you can hear many performances of it on YouTube.

And you can hear a lovely, tasteful version of *St. Louis Tickle* played (in 2015) by some of our favourite New Orleans-based musicians here:

https://www.youtube.com/watch?v=ZK8rhXX2rpk

This is a most delightful performance. May I urge you to watch it? Listen out for the 'Buddy Bolden' theme at 55 seconds.

'EGYPTIAN ELLA'

I had never heard of the song *Egyptian Ella* until 2012 when on YouTube I came across some of the New Orleans street bands performing it. The music appeals to me because the Chorus (32 bars, structured a - a - b - a) is a moderately fast, catchy tune with the 'a' section tumbling down the chromatic scale. Also it's a tune in a minor key and we don't get enough of those in traditional jazz. There are plenty of versions of it on YouTube but beware: some of them do not include the Verse.

This song is very much of its time. It would not be considered 'politically correct' today. But it is fun.

It was written in 1931 by Walter Doyle who was a popular vaudeville composer. I guess he wrote the words as well as the tune. He also composed *Mysterious Mose*, which is still sometimes heard.

As well as its 32-bar chorus, *Egyptian Ella* has a 24-bar verse – which bands should include if they have a singer, as it sets the scene with regard to Ella's biography.

The words tell the story of a dancer called Ella who 'started getting fat'. She soon got the sack and also 'lost her fella'. So she went off to Egypt and started a new life. But she found they liked fat dancers there! So she is now a big star. 'She weighs two twenty but they don't care; they like 'em plenty that way out there'. When she dances by the River Nile, 'the boys all take their old sweethearts and throw 'em to the crocodiles'! 'How they love Egyptian Ella!'

W. C. HANDY (AND ME!)

Only once in my life have I been to Memphis, Tennessee. That was on 17 October 2016. Naturally, I headed to Beale Street. And of course I had to be photographed with the statue of the great William Christopher Handy.

I also enjoyed seeing the small, unpretentious single-storey house where he lived for the eight years during which he led his own band playing on Beale Street, and wrote some of his best-known work, establishing the importance of the 12-bar blues. In fact, a few recordings of Handy and his Memphis Orchestra, made in 1917, still exist (you can find them on YouTube).

The house was originally located at 659 Janette Street, but was transported in 1983 to a new site tucked away just behind Beale Street, near the statue.

Handy lived from 1873 to 1958. Apart from being a trumpet-player and band-leader, he is best known as a composer - 'The Father of the Blues'. Among his compositions are some of the most enduring pieces in the traditional jazz repertoire: *Memphis Blues*, *St. Louis Blues*, *Beale Street Blues*, *Ole Miss Rag*, *Chantez Les Bas*, *Atlanta Blues*, *Yellow Dog Blues*, and *Aunt Hagar's Blues*.

SECTION 5: CONSIDERING THE TUNES

My guess is that there must be at least three thousand tunes that are still regularly played by traditional jazz bands. I want to invite you to think about just a tiny sample of tunes and CDs. I find these interesting, whether because of the history of the pieces or the ways in which they are performed.

'MEMPHIS SHAKE'

This tune was recorded in 1926 by a group known as *The Dixieland Jug Blowers* in Chicago. Though called a 'jug' band, they had such instruments as trombone, piano and saxophone in their line-up. What made their recording of 'Memphis Shake' special was that the great clarinettist Johnny Dodds was sitting in with them, and his contribution is very effective on the old recording. (You can hear it on You Tube.)

Not much is known about *The Dixieland Jug Blowers*. It seems to have been a short-term amalgamation of two early 'jug' bands - run respectively by old-timer Earle McDonald (banjo and jug) and Clifford Hayes (violin). It is believed that Clifford Hayes was the composer of 'Memphis Shake'.

Actually, it's not so much a tune as a simple sequence of chords that are an effective basis for improvisation. The tune has a four-bar introduction and then is in two parts.

There is a YouTube video of Tuba Skinny making a great job of this tune. I hope you will enjoy it:

https://www.youtube.com/watch?v=YT4auXXSvgQ

'LILY OF THE VALLEY'

Being an octogenarian Englishman who likes traditional jazz and has a go at playing it, I wish I could occasionally give more praise to our elderly British bands. But I have to face the harsh truth: we (I include myself) are *just not good enough*.

It's not surprising that our audiences are sparse and that young people don't come to hear us. Our music is often so dull, complacent, predictable, repetitive in format, uncreative and poorly presented. Far from swinging, it is often plodding and tedious.

Here's an example. I recently witnessed one of the well-known English bands playing *Lily of The Valley* - a fairly simple three-chorder. The tempo was so slow and the drumming weary, heavy and laboured. At times the tune threatened to drag even more. Compared with the great young musicians in New Orleans today, these players (though they possibly played better years ago) seemed to have limited technical skills. The interplay at the start was uninteresting. The usual dreary succession of 32-bar 'solos' then followed, while the musicians themselves did not look at all enthused. The banjo solo (really necessary?), though accurately working through all 32 bars - was very basic.

Compare this with a performance of the same tune in Royal Street, New Orleans:

https://www.youtube.com/watch?v=KMZGvF6Hwc4

These youngsters set and maintain a bright, foot-tapping tempo. They find a great deal to 'say' about the music. Starting - unusually - with the trombone taking the melody, they follow up with much creative interweaving involving the cornet, clarinet and trombone. Instead of tedious 32-bar 'solos', there is much exciting ensemble work, sometimes with the cornet and sometimes the clarinet taking the lead. Simple the tune may be, but some of the improvisations are astonishing. The tuba is intelligently used to provide variety and give some respite to the others before they return for a glorious ensemble finish during which there is some remarkable invention and exciting off-beat cymbal-work. They even do something unusual to end: they play the first 16 bars twice.

I hate to sound unkind. But the truth is I would rather spend my time listening to interesting and exciting performances of this quality than to performances by us elderly British musicians.

REPERTOIRE OF TUBA SKINNY

Tuba Skinny has built up an extraordinary repertoire so different from that of hundreds of other trad bands who go on playing the same old *Bill Bailey*, *All of Me* and *Muskrat Ramble* month in, month out.

Tuba Skinny's programmes mostly comprise exciting unfamiliar gems they have unearthed from the 1920s and 1930s. *Tuba Skinny* must have spent a great deal of time researching tunes that risked falling into obscurity. Their own Twenty-First Century versions manage both to show respect for the originals and yet at the same time present the tunes in a fresh and exciting manner.

My estimate is that – on YouTube – they have been filmed playing at least 300 different tunes. Some of special interest or rarity are these:

All I Want is a Spoonful (Papa Charlie Jackson 8-bar theme from 1925)

Almost Afraid to Love (On their CD *Blue Chime Stomp*. Composed by Ann Turner for Georgia White 1938)

Banjoreno (on their CD *Rag Band*) (H. Clifford, 1926, for the Dixieland Jug Blowers)

Biscuit Roller (on their CD *Rag Band*) (1937, Richard M. Jones and Georgia White)

Blue Chime Stomp (On their CD *Blue Chime Stomp*. Shaye Cohn, 2015)

Blue Devil Blues (possibly Sara Martin and her Jug Band 1925)

Bumblebee (recorded by Memphis Minnie in 1930)

Carpet Alley Breakdown (Cal Smith and Henry Clifford. Recorded by Johnny Dodds, 1926)

Cold Mornin' Shout (on their CD *Pyramid Strut*) (Bobby Leecan for The South Street Trio, 1926)

Crazy Blues (written by Perry Bradford, 1927)

Crow Jane (on their CD *Rag Band*) (Skip James, 1931)

Dallas Rag (on their CD *Owl Call Blues*; Dallas String Band, 1927)

Dreaming The Hours Away (Will E. Dulmage, 1927. Recorded 1928 by Clarence Williams' Jazz Kings)

Fingering With Your Fingers (Created by The Mississippi Sheiks in 1935)

Fourth Street Mess Around (composed by Will Shade for The Memphis Jug Band, 1930)

Freight Train Blues (on their CD *Pyramid Strut;* Recorded 1924 by Clara Smith. Composers: Thomas A Dorsey & Everett Murphy)

Frisco Bound (a 10-bar blues! Composed by Memphis Minnie and Kansas Joe in 1929)

Frog Hop (Composer : Clifford Hayes, 1929. Recorded by Clifford Hayes' Louisville Stompers that year)

Gladiolus Rag (Scott Joplin, 1907)

Harlem's Araby (Fats Waller, Porter Grainger, Jo Trent, 1924)

Hilarity Rag (James Scott, 1910)

History of Man (Trinidad calypso. T.A. Codallo, 1938; - recorded by Codallo's Top Hatters Orchestra)

I'll See You in the Spring (Memphis Jug Band, 1927)

Jackson Stomp (on their CD *Rag Band*) (Charlie McCoy and Walter Vincson, 1930, for the Mississippi Mud Steppers)

Jazz Battle (Jabbo Smith, 1929)

Jubilee Stomp (Duke Ellington, 1928)

225

Me and My Chauffeur (On their CD *Blue Chime Stomp*. Written by E. Lawler and recorded 1941 by Memphis Minnie)

Michigander Blues (Jabbo Smith, 1929)

Mississippi River Blues (Big Bill Broonzy, 1934. Tuba Skinny sometimes announce this as 'Big Boat' - the title under which the identical song was later recorded by Washboard Sam).

Nigel's Dream (Shaye Cohn, 2015)

Oriental Jazz (a.k.a. 'Oriental Rag' and 'Soudan'. On their CD *Blue Chime Stomp*. Composer: Gabriel Šebek. Recorded 1917 by the ODJB)

Postage Stomp (Sam Goble and Vic Johnston, 1930)

Russian Rag (George L. Cobb, 1918. On their CD *Rag Band*)

Skid-Dat-De-Dat (on their CD *Pyramid Strut*) (Lil Hardin, 1926)

Them Has Been Blues (by Will. E. Skidmore & Marshall Walker; recorded by Bessie Smith in 1925)

Thoughts (Robin Rapuzzi, 2015)

Tricks Ain't Walkin' No More (on their CD *Rag Band*) (Lucille Bogan song from 1930)

Variety Stomp (On their CD *Blue Chime Stomp*. Joe Trent, Ray Henderson, Bud Green, 1927)

What If We Do? (Recorded by Katherine Henderson with Clarence Williams 1930)

What's the Matter With the Mill? (Memphis Minnie and Joe McCoy, 1930)

25)

You Can Have My Husband (on their CD *Six Feet Down*) (Dorothy Labostrie, 1960)

'FRISCO BOUND' AND MEMPHIS MINNIE

Memphis Minnie was quite somebody. She could play the guitar and sing well. But she was also a composer of some fine early jazz tunes.

Her real name was Lizzie Douglas and she was born in the New Orleans suburb of Algiers in 1897. Her family later lived in Tennessee. As a child, she mastered the banjo and guitar. She took to busking in the Beale Street, Memphis, area when she was only a teenager, and she also toured with a circus. It was a hard life. She became a tough, street-wise young woman; and this toughness was reflected later in her singing and playing.

She married three times. Her second husband, Joe McCoy, was a fellow busker. They were talent-spotted and went on to make records for both Columbia and Vocalion.

It was at that time (when she was already more than 30 years old) that the publicists decided to call her 'Memphis Minnie' and the name stuck. (Similarly, her husband was given the name 'Kansas Joe'.) Between 1929 and 1934, they recorded about 30 songs, some of them more than once. After they divorced, she recorded many more, sometimes with Kansas Joe's brother and later with her third husband - Ernest Lawler ('Little Son Joe'). At this time she was mainly based in Chicago.

Minnie recorded more than 130 songs in total, several of them composed by herself. Among songs Minnie recorded that have influenced and been revived by the young New Orleans musicians of the 21st Century are: *Bumble Bee, Frisco Town, I'm Goin' Back Home, Me and My Chauffeur, Ice Man, Tricks Ain't Walkin' No More, What's The Matter With the Mill?, New Dirty Dozen,* and *When the Levee Breaks.*

227

Minnie is known to have been the composer of the following songs that she recorded: *Black Cat Blues, You Caught Me Wrong Again, Down in the Alley, Good Biscuits, Good Morning, Has Anyone Seen My Man?, Hoodoo Lady, I Hate To See The Sun Go Down, I'm a Bad Luck Woman, I've Been Treated Wrong, Ice Man, If You See My Rooster, Keep On Eating, Ma Rainey, Man You Won't Give Me No Money, My Baby Don't Want Me No More, My Butcher Man, My Strange Man, Nothin' In Rambling*. Some of the other songs for which she became well known (such as *Bumble Bee* and *Me and My Chauffeur*) were written by McCoy or Lawler.

Listen here to Minnie and her third husband (the composer) performing *Me and My Chauffeur*:

https://www.youtube.com/watch?v=KiRoNuw5x4M

And then watch the young musicians of today performing the song:

https://www.youtube.com/watch?v=kRj7sAJy7rY

Memphis Minnie seems to have been the composer of *Frisco Town* (a ten-bar blues) in 1929. She recorded it with her husband Kansas Joe the same year. Its title rapidly changed to *Frisco Bound.* (This a quite different song from the *Frisco Bound* composed by Sam Powers in 1915.)

Still in 1929, a recording of *Frisco Bound* was made by James Wiggins and this increased its popularity.

This song also has recently been revived in its ten-bar form:

https://www.youtube.com/watch?v=4KkSC7bU8co

228

'THE GREEN LEAVES OF SUMMER'

In the U.K., *The Green Leaves of Summer* was made famous in the 1960s by Kenny Ball and his Band. (Sadly, Kenny died on 7 March 2013.) Their version (available on You Tube) has it in F minor; and later (when the trombone takes over the lead) they step up a tone to G minor.

What a great little tune it is! It sounds simple enough, but its special effect is due to its unique progression largely through minor chords.

It was written for the film *The Alamo* in 1960 by the great American (Russian emigré) film composer Dimitri Tiomkin. What a lot of fine music he had to his credit!

'GRAVIER STREET BLUES'

The year was 1954 and I had just started discovering the wonderful early New Orleans-style jazz music coming to us on recordings from America. One of the first - what a great introduction to the heady effects of raw New Orleans jazz! - was *Gravier Street Blues*, composed by Clarence Williams in 1924 and played by Johnny Dodds and His Orchestra. The recording was made in 1940. I have recently learned Johnny recorded it, in fact, just two months before he died.

This tune - though largely made up of simple riffs played in a 'bluesy' manner - galvanized my interest in this branch of music. I loved the combination of Johnny's clarinet with Natty Dominique's cornet.

On the recording, there are, incidentally, good solo choruses from Johnny himself and from Lonnie Johnson on guitar.

As was often the case in the days of 78rpm recordings, the whole piece is completed in about two and a half minutes - a lesson to us all in the impact value of brevity.

A gentleman called Andy Wolfenden has generously put this recording on YouTube for us all to enjoy. So please see whether you can share my enthusiasm:

https://www.youtube.com/watch?v=Cm6i8qTQcdk

'CRAZY BLUES'

My friend Jan, who lives in Holland, is a keen gardener and also a fan of Tuba Skinny. He is particularly fond of Erika's wonderful singing. He likes to work in his garden, with Erika singing to him.

Jan has told me how much he likes *Crazy Blues* - a 2014 addition to Tuba Skinny's repertoire. Jan admires the way Erika sings almost continuously through the entire 4½-minute performance. He says he considers it a 'masterpiece' because of the the beauty of the song, the way Erika conveys the emotions and the perfect cooperation of the band in supporting Erika - without any instrumental solos.

Crazy Blues was composed in 1920 by 27-year-old Perry Bradford, who at the time was the musical director of the great early blues singer Mamie Smith. She recorded it that year with her *Jazz Hounds*. It was a hugely successful recording and is now considered by jazz and blues scholars to have been an important milestone in the history of our music.

Tuba Skinny model their version very closely on Mamie Smith's. They use the same Introduction and structure. The only significant difference is that - after the long vocal - Tuba Skinny add an instrumental ensemble once through the Section I shall call (C). I suppose that, on the Mamie Smith 1920 version, limitations of available recording time prevented the band from doing anything other than rounding the tune off very quickly.

It is indeed a *tour de force* by Erika. I don't know how she memorises so many songs of this type and sings them so well, apparently with no loss of voice. And at the most emotional moments in this song, she has to hit high Ebs, which are probably at the top of her vocal range.

It's a curiously structured song, though typical of its time, I suppose. You can think of it as having 40 bars of 'Verse' leading into a 16-bar 'Chorus' (let's call the Chorus C) - making 56 bars in all. But the performers break down the 'Verse' into two parts of 28 bars (let's call that A) and 12 bars (let's call that B) respectively. Tuba Skinny plays the song entirely in the key of Eb and the structure (Introduction plus three themes) seems to me to be:

(Intro) Band Intro: 4 bars.

(A) Erika: 28-bar theme, starting at *I can't sleep at Night; I can't eat a bite....* and ending at *My love for that man will always be.*

(C) Erika: CHORUS 16 bars *Now I Got The Crazy Blues......* and ending with *I ain't had nothin' but bad news; now I got the Crazy Blues.* Note how the band again uses the *motif* from the Introduction at the end of this.

(B) Erika: 12-bar blues theme, starting at *Now I can read his letters but I sure can't read his mind.*, ending *now I see my poor love was blind.*

(B) Erika: 12-bar blues melody again, but with a different set of words, starting at *I went to the rail-road.*

(C) Erika: CHORUS 16 bars *Now I Got The Crazy Blues.*

(C) Band: CHORUS 16 bars ensemble to round it off.

As so often, we must thank the great *digitalalexa* for filming this performance so brilliantly. Watch it <u>by clicking here.</u> And more recently, *kassiniru* posted a performance filmed at The Dew Drop Hall. You can watch it <u>by clicking here.</u> As at March 2016, Erika has not recorded this song on any of the band's CDs.

Jan also kindly sent me the words:

I can't sleep at night.
I can't eat a bite
'Cause the man I love
He don't treat me right.
He makes me feel so blue.
I don't know what to do.
Sometime I sit and sigh
And then begin to cry
'Cause my best friend
Said his last goodbye.
There's a change in the ocean,
Change in the deep blue sea, my baby.
I'll tell you, folks,
There ain't no change in me.
My love for that man will always be!
Now I got the crazy blues
Since my baby went away.
I ain't got no time to lose.
I must find him today.
Now the doctor's gonna do all that he can,
But what you're gonna need is an undertaker man.
I ain't had nothin' but bad news.
Now I got the crazy blues.
Now I can read his letters--
I sure can't read his mind.
I thought he's lovin' me.
He's leavin' all the time.
Now I see my poor love was blind.
I went to the rail-road [to]

233

Hang my head on the track.
Thought about my daddy--
I gladly snatch'd it back!
Now my babe's gone and gave me the sack.
Now I've got the crazy blues
Since my baby went away.
I ain't had no time to lose.
I must find him today.
I'm gonna do like a Chinaman, Go and get some hop--
Get myself a gun, and shoot myself a cop.
Ain't had nothing but bad news.
Now I've got the crazy blues.

'MOTHER'S SON-IN-LAW'

I made a video at the French Quarter Festival of 2015 of Tuba Skinny playing *Mother's Son-in-Law*:

https://www.youtube.com/watch?v=CpXltXTTKRI

You don't have to have a hanker
To be a broker or a banker.
No sir-ee, just simply be
My mother's son-in-law.
Needn't even think of trying
To be a mighty social lion
Sipping tea, if you will be
My mother's son-in-law.
Not got the least desire
To set the world on fire.
Just wish you'd make it proper
To call my old man 'poppa'.
You don't have to sing like Bledsoe*
And you can tell the world I said so.
Can't you see you've got to be
My mother's son-in-law?

(* Jules Bledsoe - a famous Afro-American singer and the original performer of *Ol' Man River* - was 36 years old at the time when *My Mother's Son-in-Law* was written.)

The song was composed by Alberta Nichols, who had studied piano at the Louisville Conservatory. The lyrics were written by her husband, Mann Holiner. As a partnership, they wrote over 100 songs, mainly for Broadway shows. Alberta died in 1957.

The song can be performed either as *My Mother's Son-in-Law* or *Your Mother's Son-in-Law* - according to the gender of the singer.

When they recorded it for their *Garbage Man* CD in 2011, Tuba Skinny played a vigorous version in which Kiowa Wells, their guitarist at the time, featured prominently. They played the song in keys that some Bb instrument players would consider tricky, starting with several choruses (including one vocal from Erika) in E minor and then switching to A minor for the finish - with Erika singing the words for the final part of the Chorus. Watching again my video of Tuba Skinny playing the song at the French Quarter Festival in April 2015, I was struck first by the amazing energy and drive of the performance. But I then noticed it had moved on a bit since the 2011 recording. Obviously Kiowa was no longer with the band and greater prominence was given to all the other instruments, Shaye being especially busy. But more than that: I noticed that we now had not one key change, but TWO, each preceded by a 4-bar Bridge. The band started in G minor and then followed the 2011 structure by going into E minor (including a vocal) and ending (after Robin's solo) in A minor (with Erika singing in that key too). It's a truly invigorating performance.

I then checked out Billie Holiday's recording from 1933 (available on YouTube). Sure enough, her performance also went though the keys G minor, E minor and A minor - in that order. So I guess Tuba Skinny took their inspiration from that recording.

'BUDDY'S HABIT(S)'

'Buddy's Habits' (aka 'Buddy's Habit') was written in 1923, by Arnett Nelson and Charley Straight. Thanks to the generosity of the video-maker codenamed *RagtimeDorianHenry*, you can see the sheet music and hear the piece played on the piano here:

https://www.youtube.com/watch?v=BmnSTs3RkJw

And you can hear the original recording by Charley Straight's own Orchestra here:

https://www.youtube.com/watch?v=ddTfIvA5kho

The joint composer, Arnett 'King Mutt' Nelson, was a clarinet and saxophone player. He was born in Gulfport on 8th March, 1890 and died on 14th March, 1959. His first job was with the band of John Collins, Lee Collins' father, around 1907. Arnett moved to Chicago in 1914 and is not known to have returned. He was a member of Jimmy Wade's band in Chicago and New York, 1922-27, and was in pick-up bands with Punch Miller in the late 1920s and early 1930s. He later worked with Chicago blues bands.

The other joint-composer, Charley Straight, was born in Chicago, Illinois in January 1891. He apparently had Bix Beiderbecke in his band for four months in 1925, but fired him! Charley Straight started his musical career in the early 1910s as a solo piano player and by circa 1917 led his first band. Charley's important contribution to the piano roll industry should also be noted. His early career was on the vaudeville circuit; during that period, from 1912 to 1914, while they worked in England, he issued with his partner Gene Greene several double-faced records. Shortly thereafter he became Musical Director of the Imperial Piano Roll Company (later to become QRS, the most prolific piano roll manufacturer in the world), where he made numerous rolls, collaborating with Roy Bargy on quite a few. According to *The Music Trade Review*, he left Imperial shortly before January 1922 and his piano roll activities appear to have ceased around 1926. Although his was basically a hotel dance band, Straight appreciated jazz and some of his recordings for Paramount are considered to be among the best jazz records made by a white band in the early 1920's. Straight didn't record after August 1928 but remained active as a bandleader until his death on September 2, 1940 when he was hit by a speeding car in Chicago.

The recording of 'Buddy's Habits' by Charley Straight's Orchestra was made in June 1923 and then - as 'Buddy's Habit' - it was recorded by King Oliver's Jazz Band (25 Oct 1923). Other early recordings were by The Midway Dance Orchestra (5 Dec 1923), The Bucktown Five [with Muggsy Spanier] (25 Feb 1925), Red Nichols & His Five Pennies (20 Dec 1926).

The 'Buddy' of the title was not Buddy Bolden. It was a tuba-player, Louis 'Buddy' Gross, whose habit was retiring to the rest room at the end of each set because of the vast quantity of beer he had consumed. Another 'habit' was that he got so drunk that he fell off-stage backwards, with his tuba. It seems he was a member of Charley Straight's Orchestra.

When clarinettist Arnett Nelson (the other co-composer) played in Jimmy Wade's Orchestra at the Moulin Rouge Café (Wabash Ave, Chicago), the tuba/bass sax player was also Louis 'Buddy' Gross. He recorded with Wade's Moulin Rouge Orchestra in Dec 1923 and Feb 1924.

This leaves me guessing that Arnett Nelson and Louis 'Buddy' Gross played in both Jimmy Wade's Orchestra AND Charley Straight's Orchestra in 1923. This is surely probable.

There is also a party-piece for banjo players (you can find it on YouTube) called 'Take Your Pick', with the composer credited as Pete Mandell, the banjoist with the Savoy Orpheans in London, England. This was copyrighted in 1925. 'Take Your Pick' was recorded by the Savoy Havana Band, with Pete Mandell on banjo. 'Take Your Pick' - apparently considered something of a tour-de-force in the banjo-playing fraternity - seems to be a plagiarised 'Buddy's Habits'. If there was plagiarism, the dates suggest it was from west to east.

'Buddy's Habits', which has three themes, is interesting, 'catchy' and not too challenging to play, so it is hardly surprising it quickly went the rounds and is still very popular among the bands of today.

'BURGUNDY STREET BLUES'

One of the great classics of the traditional jazz canon is *Burgundy Street Blues* - a sequence of exquisitely beautiful 12-bar blues choruses created in 1944 by George Lewis. Most clarinet players ever since have aspired to play it as a party piece. You can hear George himself playing it in a version running for just under three minutes here:

https://www.youtube.com/watch?v=tKL-RJDPH3w

And now we find the great Shaye Cohn playing *Burgundy Street Blues* as a CORNET feature with Tuba Skinny.

Is there nothing that young lady cannot do? You can watch Shaye's performance (well recorded by the video-maker codenamed *RaoulDuke504*) here:

https://www.youtube.com/watch?v=iPg- 3-ifXw

George Lewis - and clarinet players generally - play this tune in the key of C. As she does with all the vintage tunes in her repertoire, Shaye plays it in her own way, without slavish imitation. She has also brought it down to the key of F, where it is more comfortable for the cornet's range and where it still sounds exquisitely beautiful. The Tuba Skinny version runs for over six minutes - filled out with a couple of improvised choruses from each of the saxophone and clarinet, and one from the banjo.

'BLUE DRAG'

I learn something new about traditional jazz every day. Recently I learned there is a good simple tune called *Blue Drag*. It seems to have been composed in 1932 by a Russian-born composer of film scores called Josef Myrow (1910 - 1987). He was a graduate of the Curtis School of Music and an extremely good pianist. His best-remembered song is perhaps *You Make Me Feel So Young*.

I watched a YouTube of *The Thrift Set Orchestra* (of Austin, Texas), playing *Blue Drag*. In this delightful video, the vocal is sung by Albanie Falletta and the band includes some familiar faces - players who are among the best in the world today. Here it is:

https://www.youtube.com/watch?v=8lFd7sA9xck

It seemed to me this is a very good tune for bands to include in their programmes. It's good to have a 'riffy' one occasionally, especially if, like this, it is in a minor key.

Blue Drag reminds me a little of *Bei Mir Bist Du Schoen*. But it makes a good alternative to that tune for use in concerts. The two songs seem to have a very similar harmonic pattern and the same structure: a a b a, with b (the Middle Eight) providing a perfect contrast to the riff.

Even though this catchy number is new to me, perhaps some of you have known it for years. I find it was recorded long ago by such artists as Earl Hines, Freddie Taylor and Django Reinhardt.

'DANGEROUS BLUES' - AND A SAD TALE

There is so much joy in the history of traditional jazz. But frequently it is intermingled with sadness. Here's a poignant example.

Dangerous Blues was recorded by The Original Dixieland Jazz Band in 1921. You can find the recording on YouTube. In more recent times, the tune has been revived by Tuba Skinny. You can hear them playing it here:

https://www.youtube.com/watch?v=hE4wMgDXahk

It's a merry enough tune. But here's the sad tale behind it. The composer of this tune, Billie Brown, was a young lady who died of smallpox very soon after she composed it.

We know that is correct. But unfortunately not much else is known for sure about Billie. Billie was probably born in 1903 and became something of a child prodigy. She first had some music published when she was only 12 years old. In the next few years, six more of her songs were published. Billie's mother, Anna Welker Brown (who lived on until 1935), wrote lyrics to most of Billie's tunes, including the words for *Dangerous Blues*.

Billie's first song was published in Kansas City, and she is believed to have been living there with her mother in a rooming house at the time. One record suggests her mother may have been a music teacher (presumably she taught Billie) and that Billie worked as a pianist in a cafeteria. This was a time in history when it was still normal for children at such an age to have jobs rather than be in school.

By the time of *Dangerous Blues*, Billie had secured a job as a composer and pianist (piano and song demonstrator) for the J. W. Jenkins Music Company - a large and prosperous musical instrument dealer and music publisher. As well as *Dangerous Blues*, Jenkins published her *Lonesome Mama Blues* and *Lullaby Moon* - both very popular at the time - and also composed in 1921.

Dangerous Blues was a great success and Billie received a good deal of money from royalties during the weeks before she died. As we know, both the blues singer Mamie Smith and The Original Dixieland Jazz Band immediately picked the tune up and recorded it.

And then - how awful! - poor young Billie contracted smallpox and by December 4th she was dead. What a terrible loss to the development of our music.

Another of Billie's songs - *What's On Your Mind* - was published posthumously.

No sure evidence concerning Billie's father has been found, but he may have died earlier. Her mother Anna re-married when Billie was about 16 years old.

The crazy lyrics of *Dangerous Blues* appear to be:
Ta de da da de dum. Ta de da da de dum.
There's a funny strain a'stealing through my brain
It drives me 'most insane it seems.
Ta de da da de dum. Ta de da da de dum.
If you listen now, I'll tell you what this
Ta da da de-dum means:
CHORUS:
Oh, I got them dangerous blues.
Naughty dog-gone dangerous blues.
Can't you hear the music playing soft and sweet?
It's the kind that makes you want to shake your feet.
I think I'm slippin'; I know I'm slippin'.
Ta de da de da de da de da de da de dum.

Weary, dreary dangerous blues;
they're the kind you hate to lose.
I can't even think,
So lay me out in pink.
Every time that saxophone it moans
I want to sink.
'Cause I got them dog-gone dangerous blues.
Oh, I got them dangerous blues.
Naughty dog-gone dangerous blues.
Can't you hear the music playing soft and sweet?
It's the kind that makes you want to shake your feet.
I think I'm slippin'; I know I'm slippin'.
Ta de da de da de da de da de da de dum.
Weary, dreary dangerous blues;
they're the kind you hate to lose.
I can't even think,
Can't even sleep a wink.
Every time I hear those mournful blues
I want to sink.
'Cause I got them dog-gone dangerous blues.

By the way, a researcher found records of a couple living in Eureka Springs, whose names were William B. Brown and Anna Welker. They adopted in about 1895 a baby with the name Irene Anderson, who is believed to have been born the previous year. The researcher suggested this could have been Billie's family and that this baby - despite her name - could have been Billie. If so, that would have made her about 27 when she died. Although this speculation may be true, it raises troubling questions. How come Billie's age was given as 18 on her death certificate? How and why did it come about that her name changed from Irene Anderson to

Billie Brown? How come she and her mother are recorded as living in Kansas City, so far (250 miles) north of Eureka Springs? Why did the William Brown in question, still living in Eureka Springs in 1930, describe himself as a widower in the Census of that year? I prefer to believe the details given on the death certificate.

'DROPPIN' SHUCKS'

My friend Jim Sterling of Florida told me he had recently been pleased to discover the video of Tuba Skinny playing *Droppin' Shucks* in Royal Street as long ago as 2012, when the band still had Ryan Baer on banjo and when there was no reed player. I'm talking of this video:

https://www.youtube.com/watch?v=ZZUcZ4FmFcQ

The message from Jim reminded me that I enjoyed the video when I first saw it. At the time, I remember listening also (for comparison) to the original 1926 version composed by Lil Hardin Armstrong and recorded by Louis Armstrong's Hot Five (also available on YouTube).

But on that occasion, apart from feeling that it was a good but quite complicated piece of music, I thought no more about it.

Jim enjoyed the performance and particularly praised Shaye's muted cornet work. Throughout the three minutes, Shaye uses her Humes and Berg 102 stone-lined cup mute and has it fully wedged inside the bell of her cornet. We know that on other occasions, she prefers to hold it half in and half out of the bell. Barnabus also, using his Humes and Berg stone-lined straight mute, plays some lovely stuff complementing Shaye's melodic lines. Jim also specially liked the final Chorus, in which Shaye and Barnabus play so well together, alternating the 'breaks'.

It's interesting to observe how Ryan (at 2 mins 08 secs) warns Max that the band is about to go to the 12-bar 'breaks interlude' rather than the start of the Chorus; and then (at 2 mins 24 secs) that this time they are returning to the start of the Chorus. (The 'Breaks Interlude' is copied from the original Armstrong recording.) Perhaps Max hadn't played this number with the band before. (In fact it is a song they seem to have played very rarely over the years.)

Now that Jim has encouraged me to listen more carefully to it again, I realise *Droppin' Shucks* is not really as complicated as I had thought. Basically it has a simple and pretty 16-bar minor-key Verse played once (Tuba Skinny play it in C minor); and then the Chorus - played several times (in the key of Ab) - is simply one of those 16-bar standards (with 'breaks' on Bars 9 - 12), very similar to *How Come You Do Me Like You Do Do Do?* or *If It Don't Fit, Don't Force It* or *Don't Care Blues* or *Don't Go Away, Nobody*, or *Forget Me Not Blues*.

The only little extra ingredient is that 12-bar 'Breaks Interlude' I mentioned - which may be regarded as optional.

As for what the title *Droppin' Shucks* means, I think you may be able to find out. But I shall say nothing on the subject. I limit the contents of my pages to the decorous, the refined, and the tasteful.

ONE TUNE - TWO TITLES?

It is surprising how many tunes in the traditional jazz repertoire have with the passage of time acquired more than one title. There must have been various reasons for this, one of which was that a later performer wanted to disguise the fact that he was plagiarising a tune from an earlier band. But I am sure there were other reasons too, that had more to do with mere memory loss.

Here are over fifty examples. Maybe you can think of some more?

Algiers Strut is also *You're all I Want for Christmas*

Astoria Strut is also known as *Climax Rag*

Atlanta Blues (final strain) is also known as *Make Me a Pallet on the Floor*

Babik is a variation on *I Got Rhythm*

Barnyard Blues is also known as *Livery Stable Blues*

Black Bottom Stomp is also known as *Queen of Spades*

Blame it on the Blues is also known as *Quincy Street Stomp*

Bluebells Goodbye is also known as *Bright Eyes Goodbye*

Bogalusa Strut is a re-interpretation of the first two strains of Scott Joplin's *Rose Leaf Rag*

Bugle Boy March is also known as *American Soldier*

California Blues is also known as *Blue Yodel No. 4*

Can I Sleep in Your Arms Tonight, Lady? is the same tune as *Red River Valley* and is the same tune as *We Shall Walk Through the Streets of the City*

Chant of the Tuxedos is virtually the same as *Ol' Man Mose*

Chicago Breakdown is the same as *Stratford Hunch*

Chimes Blues is also known as *Mournful Serenade*

Creole Love Call is basically the middle theme from *Camp Meeting Blues*

Creole Song is also known as *L'Autre Can Can* and is also known as *Madame Pedoux*

Dauphine Street Blues (first strain) is also known as *Nobody Knows the Way I Feel This Morning*

Deep Bayou Blues is also known as *The Three Sixes*

Dippermouth Blues was re-created by the Fletcher Henderson Orchestra as *Sugarfoot Stomp*

Do Lord (tune) is also known as *It Takes a Worried Man to Sing a Worried Song*

Don't Go 'Way, Nobody (tune) is also known as *How Come You Do Me Like You Do Do Do?* and is also known as *Everybody's Talking About Sammy* and is also known as *I'm a Ding Dong Daddy from Dumas* and is also known as *If It Don't Fit, Don't Force It* and is much the same as *Walk Right In*

Don't You Feel My Leg is also known as *Don't Make Me High*

Down Home Rag is also known as *Black Rag*

Duke's Place is also known as *C-Jam Blues*

Fidgety Feet is also known as *War Clouds*

Frogimore Rag (trio) is also *Sweetheart of Mine*

Frosty Morning Blues is also known as *Lost Your Man Blues*

The Eyes of Texas (tune) is also known as *I've Been Working on the Rail-road*

Garbage Man Blues is also known as *Call of the Freaks* and is also known as *New Call of the Freaks*

Get a Working Man is identical to *Pinchbacks, Take 'Em Away* (and the chorus is harmonically the same as *It's a Long Way to Tipperary*)

Golden Leaf Strut is also known as *Milenberg Joys*

Good Time Flat Blues is also known as *Farewell to Storyville*

Hesitating Blues is also known as *How Long, How Long Blues*

Hiawatha Rag is also known as *A Summer Idyll*

San Jacinto Stomp is based on *You Can't Escape from Me* and is also known as *In the Groove* and is also known as *Baby, I Don't Mean Maybe* and is harmonically identical to *The Kat's Got Kittens*

I Hope Gabriel Likes My Music is also known as *I Hope You Like My Music*

In The Highways (I'll Be Somewhere Working for My Lord) is pretty much the same as *Down By The Riverside*

In The Sweet By and By is also known as *The Preacher and the Slave*

Joe Avery's Piece is also known as *Victory Walk* and also as *The New Second Line*

La Harpe Street Blues (theme) is also known as *We Sure Do Need Him Now*

Lily of the Valley is also known as *Everybody Ought To Know* and was probably plagiarized from the final theme of *Red Onion Drag*

London Blues is also known as *Shoe Shiner's Drag*

Lotus Blossom is also known as *Sweet Lotus Blossom* (it started out as *Sweet Marijuana*, of course; but that title came to be considered politically incorrect)

Loveless Love is also known as *Careless Love*

Love Me Tender is also known as *Aura Lee*

Martha is also known as *Mazie*

Memphis Blues is also known as *Mr. Crump*

Milneberg Joys is usually mis-spelt *Milenberg Joys* [The New Orleans suburb took its name from Scotsman Alexander Milne]

Midnight Mama - see under *Tom Cat Blues*

Mississippi Wobble is also known as *Quality Shout*

Montmartre is also known as *Django's Jump*

Mood Indigo is also known as *Dreamy Blues*

Moonlight and Roses is actually *Lemare's 'Andantino'*

New Orleans Bump is also known as *Monrovia*

Old Stack o'Lee Blues (not Stack o'Lee Blues) is virtually identical to *Faraway Blues*

Oriental Jazz was called *Soudan* by its composer

The 1919 March is also known as *The Rifle Rangers*

China Boy is also known as *Pacific Rim Stomp*

Poor Old Joe is also known as *Old Black Joe*

Lazy Luke (composed in 1905 by George J. Philpot) was misleadingly renamed *Red Flannel Rag* by Turk Murphy when he recorded it many years later

Moanful Blues is actually *Some Day Sweetheart*

My Good Man Sam is virtually identical to *Doctor Jazz*

After You've Gone (1917) seems to have plagiarized *Peg o' My Heart* (1913)

Riverboat Shuffle was originally *Free Wheeling*

Riverside Blues is also known as *Dixieland Shuffle*

Root Hog or Die is virtually the same as *Bei Mir Bist Du Schoen*

The final theme of *Royal Garden Blues* is also the main theme of *Georgia Bo Bo*

Savoyager's Stomp is also known as *Muskrat Ramble*

Sidewalk Blues is also known as *Fishtail Blues*

251

Silver Bell (second theme) is also known as *Sometimes My Burden's Too Hard to Bear*

Si Tu Vois Ma Mère is also known as *Lonesome*

Soap Suds is also known as *Fickle Fay Creep*

South is also known as *Pork Chop*

Storyville Blues is also known as *Those Drafting Blues* and is also known as *Bienville Blues*

Gully Low Blues is also known as *S.O.L. Blues*

Original Dixieland One-Step (final strain) is also known as *That Teasing Rag*

Take My Hand, Precious Lord is the same tune as *Maitland*

Tar Paper Stomp is also known as *Hot and Anxious* (one theme) and is also known as *In The Mood*

The Midnight Special is also known as *Shine a Light on Me*

Till Times Get Better and *Smokehouse Blues* are almost identical to *Up a Lazy River*

Ting-a-ling started its life as *Waltz of the Bells*

Tom Cat Blues is also known as *Midnight Mama (or Midnight Papa)* and is also known as *Nobody Knows The Way I Feel This Morning LINKED TO Winin' Boy Blues*

Two Nineteen Blues is also known as *Mamie's Blues*

Uptown Bumps was originally *The Long Lost Blues* (by Paul Wyer, 1914). Its final theme is also known as *The Bucket's Got a Hole in It*. It also became *Keep a Knockin' But You Can't Come In*. *The Bucket's Got a Hole in It* is also known as *Ta-Wa-Bac-A-Wa*.

Viper Mad is also known as *Pleasure Mad*

Washington and Lee Swing is also known as *Tulane Swing* and *Louisiana Swing*

Way Down upon the Swanee River is also known as *The Old Folks at Home*

Weary Blues is also known as *Travelling Blues* and much of it is often played as *Shake It And Break It* (but note there is also a different *Shake It And Break It* recorded by King Oliver)

When Shadows Fall is also known as *Home*

Yaaka Hula Hickey Dula is also known as *Hawaiian Love Song*

BUT:

Please note that Red Onion Rag (by Abe Olman, 1912) is a quite different tune from Louis Dumaine's *Red Onion Drag.*

SECTION 6: MY CODA

I will sign off with some miscellaneous thoughts. Happy listening!

YOUR FIRST VISIT TO NEW ORLEANS?

You're planning a holiday in New Orleans? It will be your first time there? Great. You will love it.

My friend and keen video-maker James Sterling from Florida has visited New Orleans more often than I have; and he passed on to me his own recommendations. He says you should get out of the French Quarter occasionally, particularly by using the St. Charles Streetcar which will quickly take you to the Garden District, with its stately mansions, hotels and restaurants, as well as the fine Audubon Park and Zoo. Then there is Magazine Street. You can visit it while in the Garden District. It is lined with quirky shops, pubs and eateries and is just a five-block walk from the streetcar line. That is a very good tip - not one that many people would think of.

And James enjoyed the World War II Museum in the Warehouse District, just up-river from the French Quarter. In addition to the displays, it has a theatre with live revues of music from the WWII era.

For a place to stay, James likes the many bed-and-breakfast inns. He says: 'You will get a private room usually in an old mansion with personal service from the inn-keeper and will meet new friends around the breakfast table.'

There are indeed plenty of hotels and other forms of accommodation. Imagine you stay at a hotel in Burgundy Street, somewhere near the junction with St. Ann Street. The best way to get around in the French Quarter, where most of the jazz is to be heard, will be on foot. The entire French Quarter is small - only about half a square mile in total. It will be a mere 5-minute walk to

255

Preservation Hall, or 12 minutes to the Palm Court Jazz Café. It will take you only 15 minutes to walk to Frenchmen Street, which is just beyond the French Quarter at its north-eastern edge; and there in the evenings (and some afternoons) you will find such great bars and clubs as the *dba*, *The Maison* and *The Spotted Cat*, where some wonderful bands regularly play.

From 11 a.m. daily, you will be able to hear great busking groups if you head to Royal Street (five minutes on foot from you hotel).

You will of course enjoy sampling all the other amazing things the French Quarter has to offer, including plenty of fine eating places. You must have a stroll by the Mississippi – maybe heading down to the Riverwalk Shopping Mall, which I like very much (a great place for buying shoes, in my experience!). On the way to it, you could visit the Audubon Aquarium of the Americas. On another day, head left alongside the river to a different kind of shopping experience – the famous and massive French Market. I always buy a souvenir 'New Orleans Jazz' baseball cap there; and the prices are the lowest in town.

Of course you will dawdle among the artists in Jackson Square (where there is usually also some lively jazz busking).

And you may visit special events at The Mint, or take rides on the streetcars to the Garden District or the huge City Park, or have a river trip on the *Natchez*. Or you might care to cross the River on the ferry to Algiers. Maybe you will go on one of those 'Bayou' tours or a 'Cemetery' tour (easily bookable - you will see them widely advertised).

My advice would be to give the garish and vulgar Bourbon Street only a few minutes of your time. I suppose it's worth seeing, if only to convince yourself that such a street really exists. And you

256

will hardly be able to avoid it, as it's right there in the centre of the French Quarter. But if you are a serious traditional jazz fan, there are far better places to be.

But please don't take me as authoritative. I live 4500 miles from New Orleans and have been to the City only five times during the last 25 years, so (even with help from James) I don't claim to be an expert. I am simply giving you a few personal impressions that may be of some use.

On my first visit, when I was about 55 years old, I spent most evenings at Preservation Hall. I heard such players as Harold Dejan, Milton Batiste, Narvin Kimball, Percy Humphrey, Willie Humphrey, Danny Barker, Frank Demond, Kid Sheik Colar and the very young Greg Stafford. But in recent years I have spent my evenings in the bars and clubs of Frenchmen Street to catch the exciting new generation of great bands that have evolved in New Orleans since Hurricane Katrina.

A couple of further points:

1. Transport between the airport and the City Centre (about 15 miles) is easy. There are plenty of taxis. And some hotels run shuttle services. In 2016 a taxi cost 40 dollars (including tip) for a single trip. But there is also a regular bus service (the Jefferson Transit) which is efficient and remarkably cheap (about a couple of dollars), which I have occasionally used. Obviously get up-to-date information from the internet.

2. When is the best time to go? All the year round there is good jazz. However, bear this point in mind: in June, July and August it can be extremely hot – maybe too hot for comfort. Even some of the musicians make this the time of year when they head north and tour in cooler States, or even fly to other continents to play at festivals. The French Quarter Festival (in April) is

recommended as there is an organised programme with dozens of bands giving free concerts on temporary stages in many of the streets. However, the crowds can be huge and you may have the disappointment of not being able hear your favourite bands in the best possible conditions. Also, unsurprisingly, hotel prices tend to be quite a bit higher during festivals. So you may prefer to go at a quieter time when you will be able to spend your evenings in the bars, hearing your favourite bands in conditions that are acoustically better and less crowded.

CHATTANOOGA - AND THE CHOO CHOO

Despite its close association with Glenn Miller and his Orchestra, the song *Chattanooga Choo Choo* was actually composed for a 1941 movie by the great Harry Warren. Mack Gordon provided the words.

Warren was prolific. His compositions included, for example, *You'll Never Know, I Only Have Eyes for You, Jeepers Creepers, That's Amore, At Last, Lullaby of Broadway, You Must Have Been a Beautiful Baby, Nagasaki, I Love My Baby; My Baby Loves Me,* and *September in the Rain* - to name but a few.

I'm thinking of Chattanooga because my wife and I stayed there for just one night in October 2016. We went up the nearby Lookout Mountain on the amazing Incline Railway, opened in 1895. It runs for a whole mile and is one of the steepest passenger railways in the world.

Chattanooga itself is a pretty place, especially around the River. But the Big Feature of Chattanooga is indeed *The Chattanooga Choo Choo Hotel*. That is where we stayed.

This former railway terminus fell into disuse and might well have been bulldozed had it not been for businessmen who, starting in 1973, began redeveloping it as a hotel complex. The Booking Hall has now become a restaurant.

And where the platforms used to be, gardens and fountains have been neatly laid out.

Several trains have been kept as relics of the bygone age. Some of the carriages are furnished as hotel rooms; but there are also plenty of apartments in a block at the far end.

The Chattanooga Choo Choo itself (built in the 1890s and last used in the 1940s) is a favourite for photographs.

My wife and I greatly enjoyed our few hours in Chattanooga. It was particularly peaceful sitting in those gardens. I would have liked to play *Chattanooga Choo Choo* while I was next to the train in question, but - with lots of people looking on - I was too nervous to play more than half a dozen notes of the tune. Care to witness my feeble effort? Here it is:

https://www.youtube.com/watch?v=ORaq1wI7Mf0

A BIT OF FUN: BARBERSHOP MEETS TRADITIONAL JAZZ

When Barbershop meets Traditional Jazz: here's a possible programme. Can you think of any more ?

I wish I Could Shampoo Like My Sister Kate

Just a Closer Shave

When You Wore a Toupee

My Old Kentucky Comb

Bye Bye Black Beard

Somebody Stole My Curl

Wig Shall Not Be Moved

Joe Avery's HairPiece

Some Day You'll Be Baldy

Razors of Picardy

Whiskering

There's Soap Soap in Your Eyes

When You and I Were Young, Goatee

Moustache's Gone, Goodbye

Moonlight and Razors

Stubble in Mind

It's Only a Paper Towel

Mack the Razor

Old Barber's Chair's Got Me

My Little Gel

Ain't Ever Shavin'

You Always Cut The One You Shave

Is It True What They Say About Trichology?

SHAYE COHN

I must conclude by returning to the young lady who, however modest and unassuming, has done more than anyone else to sustain and perform our music in recent years – and always to the highest standards.

Shaye Cohn used to play a pocket trumpet before obtaining a cornet. You can see her busking powerfully and joyfully on a pocket trumpet in videos dating from 2008.

But for several years she has been associated with her long-model cornet that is surely older than Shaye herself. Its plating is worn round some of the tubes and valves, suggesting that it has had heavy use for many years. To me it looks like a YCR-234 Yamaha from the 1970s. It's the kind of cornet you could pick up on an Internet auction for about 100 dollars.

Bob Andersen of San Diego told me it formerly belonged to Ed Polcer, father of the very fine New Orleans jazz trumpeter Ben Polcer. Ed has been playing jazz cornet for 55 years!

Shaye also enjoys using mutes – especially her Humes and Berg 102 stone-lined cup mute. With this, Shaye achieves the most glorious, crisp jazzy effects.

Yet, with this modest kit Shaye has produced some of the most sublime traditional jazz to be heard in the world today. There could be no better proof that a really great performer can strut his or her stuff without recourse to expensive equipment.

Shaye is not a showy player. Not from her will you hear those screaming, raucous, high-note 32-bar solo choruses to which so many traditional jazz trumpeters resort. But she is a very energetic player of the cornet. She produces a unique tone that perfectly encapsulates the blues feeling that is at the heart of so much of our music.

Most cornet players aim to produce a beautifully clean, clear, open, round, full tone. Think of the best English brass bands. (By the way, brass bands in England - the type who participate in national contests and who perform in park bandstands during the summer - are quite different from the jazz 'brass bands' that you find in New Orleans.) The cornet players of such bands as Black Dyke, Brighouse and Rastrick, Foden's and Cory are examples of players who achieve this angelic purity of tone.

But traditional jazz cornet (and trumpet) players need a tone that is a little bit rougher and that allows for jazzy effects - bending notes, being bluesy and occasionally even rasping a little. Very few of them have much use for that sublime purity of tone common among the top English-style brass band players.

And Shaye has succeeded in developing a tone that is perfect for her 1920s style of music. It is distinctive and unique. I can't think of any other cornet player who sounds or has sounded like her. At best, I can say her tone is midway between those of George Mitchell (1899 - 1972) and Natty Dominique (1896 - 1982).

Listen closely to her busy fluent phrases, often muted and in the background, interwoven brilliantly into the polyphony of her band's wonderful music. Her contributions to ensembles remind me of the viola parts in Mozart's string quartets. (She is also great at what Punch Miller used to call 'fast fingering'.)

Shaye has said: 'One thing really important to *The Loose Marbles* was ensemble playing. When I first started with them, I was playing second trumpet. So I had to work to find a voice where I could fit in. It taught me to play very simply, and to listen'.

It is often said that Shaye inherited her talents from her father and grandfather - both of them famous in jazz history for their own contributions. There may be some truth in this, though I am sure Shaye has worked extremely hard to develop her own skills and versatility and to play the music in her own way. I also believe greater credit should be given to her mother - a very fine jazz pianist and singer who, in my opinion, may have had an even deeper influence on Shaye.

Shaye has an instinctive understanding of rhythmic possibilities, subtle and surprising harmonies and progressions, even when improvising at high speed. She can 'bend' notes to great effect and in exactly the right places.

She always works hard to encourage great teamwork from the *band*, not just to display her own skills. Her playing takes account of (and usually directs) all that is going on around her.

In fact, she seems to be the arranger of the music for *Tuba Skinny* - discovering long-forgotten gems from recordings made by jazz bands and string bands and jug-blower bands 80 - 90 years ago, and making them sound completely fresh and exciting, with all the armoury of breaks, stop chords, long-held notes, offbeat rhythms, clever introductions and codas, key changes and so on. Shaye holds all this in her head for an astonishingly wide repertoire of tunes.

Shaye also takes great care in setting tempos before a tune is started. And when a fast tempo is required, she and the band ensure it is maintained with excitement and no dragging later in the tune.

On top of all this, Shaye is a fine composer of tunes for traditional jazz bands. On YouTube you can witness performances by Tuba Skinny of her compositions *Blue Chime Stomp*, *Nigel's*

Dream, Owl   Call   Blues, Pyramid   Strut, Salamanca Blues and *Tangled Blues* - all of them fine pieces.

And that is not all. Shaye is also one of the best traditional jazz *pianists*!

She is also a fine violinist; and in 2016, she even took up playing the trombone - and played it in the all-female band that she formed.

It is impossible to account for Shaye's special cornet tone. Observe her even when she is playing without a mute: the sound is still distinctively her own.

If you are a cornet player and think you can produce a sound exactly like Shaye Cohn's, well - just try! I doubt whether you will get anywhere near it.

Most remarkable, Shaye did not even begin learning to play the cornet until she settled in New Orleans after Hurricane Katrina. Following a classical music training, she arrived in New Orleans as a player of the piano, accordion and violin.

I have not come across a traditional jazz musician who impresses me more than Shaye. She is simply the best.

About The Author

Pops Coffee

If his memory serves him correctly, Pops Coffee was – long, long ago - a lecturer in English Literature. Since his retirement, his main interest has been Traditional Jazz and learning to play it.

He is also the author of *Playing Traditional Jazz* and *Jane Austen Junket*.

Made in the USA
San Bernardino, CA
08 July 2018